Make the Connection!

Make the Connection!

A Practical Guide to Parents and Practitioners for Teaching the Nonverbal Child to Communicate - with AAC

Susan Berkowitz

M.S. CCC-SLP, M.Ed.

Make the Connection, A Practical Guide to Parents and Practitioners for Teaching the Nonverbal Child to Communicate - with AAC

©2019 Susan Berkowitz
Based on the work of Susan Berkowitz © 2018
Published by Herding Cats Press
EDITORIAL OFFICE
Blue Moon Wonders
114 C Avenue #228
Coronado, CA 92118
U.S.A.

Library of Congress Cataloging-in-Publication Data
Berkowitz, Susan
Make the Connection, A Practical Guide to Parents and Practitioners for Teaching the Nonverbal Child to Communicate – with AAC / Susan Berkowitz M.A., CCC-SLP

Editorial and production: John Seeley

Cover design: Kate Pullen
Cover photo: Bob Adams © 2018
ISBN-13: 978-1-945533-01-3
Printed in the USA on acid-free paper

This book is dedicated to all the children who need AAC and the parents and professionals who support them, and all who strive to connect, in all forms of communication.

TABLE OF CONTENTS

ACKNOWLEDGEMENTS

I want to thank my wonderfully supportive family, and the cats who warmed my lap while I wrote. I would also like to thank my editor, John Seeley, and talented artist Kate Pullen for her wonderful cover art and design.

FOREWORD

In my practice I have heard 2 different, but related, refrains over and over. On the one hand, parents have told me that they don't know how to teach their (nonspeaking) child to communicate. While they understand some of what their child wants, sometimes even mothers don't know what their child is trying to say.

It might be that they've bought or been given an iPad, but have discovered that you can't put an AAC system in front of the child and expect him to pick it up and use it. They don't know what to do next. If left without direction for too long, the parents just abandon the device, and so, too, do their children.

When I do AAC trainings in school districts, I try to have them invite parents. Sometimes it happens. But, more often it doesn't. Parents are usually unable to come to school during the day, when they've got to be at work. School staff may be unable to meet before or after school if it is outside of their contract hours. In some cases, I've had schools videotape my trainings, so that families and staff can watch when it is convenient. On the other hand, we have clinicians who are licensed SLPs but have had little or no training or experience with AAC. They lament having these students on their caseloads when they don't know how to implement the augmentative/alternative communication. Many SLPs do not get AAC coursework or experience in their graduate programs, and don't know much about it when a student shows up on their caseload. Fortunately, they are now able to find a lot of information on the internet.

Unfortunately, there is no quality control over the information available on-line, and it's not all EBP. (Evidence Based Practice)

In my private practice I have worked with public and nonpublic schools, adult day programs, group homes, and families; trying to bridge the gap between what parents and professionals need and what they have.

What I think both sides need is a practical way to consistently work together to teach their students/children to communicate competently. Hence, this book; Parents and Professionals as Partners.

Collaboration between school and home is a significant concept for students who use picture-based communication. Without both communication partners, school and home, working consistently to provide the students with the opportunities and strategies needed to become competent communicators, it probably won't happen.

There are so many opportunities that cross both environments; particularly in routines that are common. Children perform routine tasks like washing hands or eating a snack, even brushing their teeth in multiple environments. The vocabulary is consistent, the sequence is consistent, and the language used is consistent - or it should be.

There are also situations, routines, and activities that are unique to either home or school, but are highly engaging opportunities for communicating. For each of these, communication partners need to think about how to use them to build communication skills.

When it was suggested to me that I should write a book, I had envisioned writing a how-to manual for parents; who often get little or no information about how to work with AAC with their children. But then it was also suggested that I write for SLPs who may be new to AAC. So, this book is my attempt to provide information to both of those groups of communication partners, so that they can understand and implement AAC strategies and systems. I want parents and professionals to feel that they are both armed with the same basic knowledge and can work with each other in a partnership that helps their children and students become competent communicators.

What I hope you will learn from this book includes the nuts and bolts of AAC terminology, options, and implementation strategies. I also hope that the specific activity examples will provide the inspiration for caregivers and professionals to implement AAC in all environments in which the student needs to communicate. In other words; everywhere.

INTRODUCTION

I have been a speech-language pathologist for 40 years, working mostly with students with complex communication needs and with Augmentative-Alternative Communication (AAC). For the past 20 years I have run my own private consulting practice; providing independent evaluations to parents and school districts alike, and training school districts' staff in implementation strategies.

Standing out glaringly over these 20 years is the dearth of information available to parents as well as to SLPs who do not have prior experience or instruction in AAC - about how they can teach their child to communicate. While today's landscape in the field is very different from what it was 20 years ago, I still hear the same questions from parents and SLPs alike, "How do I teach this child to communicate?" "Why is the information I have been given incorrect or inefficient?" "What do I do now?" And, more recently, "The district gave this kid an iPad and an AAC app. Now what?"

Recently, I was at a convention, exhibiting my implementation resources. An SLP came up to me and told me what she had learned from a video on the internet about AAC and creating a communication system. There were a couple of problems with what she had seen. First, the symbols were variable in their location from one minute to the next, or one session to the next. Second, the array of which words were available at any given time changed. And, third, there was only a single array available at any one time; further limiting the vocabulary available to the student.

This set up makes it more difficult for the child to learn to communicate. He has to scan the array for each symbol and do so every time, in order to see what is available to him, and to see where the word he wants is now. This takes a lot of cognitive energy; energy that would be better spent formulating language.

As we spoke, and she looked at sample materials I had with me, she cried, "I've been doing it all wrong!" Well, a good many of us did it "wrong" over the years. The field of AAC is a relatively young one, and much of the relevant research has been recent. A lot of what we learned 20 or 30 years ago was not evidence based; there was little evidence, as there was little research. When I started in the field more than 40 years ago there were no standardized communication icons beyond Blissymbols; we tore pictures out of magazines. Even the manner in which we conduct assessments and implementation has undergone many changes.

This book is for all of those parents and professionals who want to "get it right," but need the guidance to get there. We know that collaboration between school and home is a significant component in the lives of students who use picture-based communication.

The information and ideas in this book are not unique; they are things I have learned over the past 40 years from articles, books, seminars and most importantly, from my students. Much of this information is available elsewhere, but not in this unique format. What I have tried to do is to curate the ideas in a way that cuts away the jargon, the discussion of research protocols; leaving all but the basic information and strategies, both groups need.

Parents often find themselves in a few distinct situations:

- They have a nonspeaking child and they don't know where to begin building communication skills.

- They have bought or been given an iPad and AAC app, but school staff say the child isn't "ready" and refuse to implement it.

- They borrow a device from a loan program (many states have them), but the trial "fails" because nobody has known how to implement teaching for a successful trial.

Professionals find themselves in some unique situations, too.

Graduate training programs are not mandated to provide instruction in AAC. Many programs don't have a professor who could teach such a class and/or provide clinical supervision.

Neither does licensure require that such training be provided as a requirement for state licensing or federal certification.

Relatively few SLPs, therefore, begin their practice with a strong background - or any background - in this area. Without being self-motivated to work in this area and acquire continuing education in AAC, SLPs just do not feel equipped to work with a nonspeaking population.

Professionals have told me that they really don't want another text book. And, quite frankly, that's not what parents need, either. The stakeholders in this partnership have told me they want a combination of easily understood information, and practical, actionable strategies they can go use tomorrow. Often, they're not even interested in the why and how of what works, only that it does and here is how you do it. They want to hit the ground running with strategies that actually work. They want to be able to look at this child and say, "I know what to do."

This book begins with presenting an overview of AAC terminology, basic premises, and systems - the What of AAC. Then it moves to practical intervention strategies for introducing AAC to children, expanding their vocabulary, syntax, and communication functions - the How and some of the Why. I will also touch very briefly on providing access to the general curriculum and literacy for AAC users.

Far too often children who are nonspeaking, or whose verbal skills are not functional to meet their needs, are not provided access to sufficient communication or to core curriculum. Educators, therapists, and even parents often underestimate the ability of these students to learn language and literacy skills. Some children are deemed "too low functioning" to benefit from alternative communication systems. Others are thought to be too young to be ready for such systems. Far too often, I have seen the "wait to see" route taken - wait to see if verbal skills develop; thus, failing to provide an alternative mode of communication while waiting.

This book will show you why these "myths" about AAC aren't true and give you practical information about how to increase communication skills in children; because lack of access to communication results in students being denied access to social relationships and academic success. Lack of access to communication results in the child being excluded from general education classrooms, restricting his social development, and ultimately restricting his quality of life.

Children need access to appropriate and effective communication modes as soon as possible. Without an appropriate way to communicate genuine messages, children frequently use inappropriate behaviors to communicate, or withdraw from even attempting to communicate.

Any child whose speech is not effective to meet his communication needs or who does not have speech is a candidate for AAC. It is our role as speech-language pathologists to "assess, intervene, and evaluate progress and outcomes associated with AAC interventions using principles of evidence-based practice, and facilitate individuals' uses of AAC to promote and maintain their quality of life."[1] In this book SLPs will learn practical assessment and intervention techniques that will assist them in meeting ASHA's suggested knowledge base in the area of AAC, and specific strategies and ideas you take can back to your classrooms, therapy rooms, and homes tomorrow.

---

[1] ASHA "The Roles and Responsibilities of Speech-Language Pathologists with Respect to AAC"

Parents will learn how to "assess" the AAC evaluation and implementation plan, and what to look for in both the AAC system and the implementation plan.

TEN BENEFITS OF READING THIS BOOK

1. Learn who should use AAC and the evidence- based research behind it.

2. Learn how to assess the AAC needs of your children/students & what you need to know as a parent about AAC evaluations: Learn current trends away from discrete skills-based assessments and towards genuine activity-based evaluation. See how to set up child-centered activities and observations to evaluate your students' skills and needs.

3. Get simple solutions you can apply to your caseload or child tomorrow: You will come away with a variety of intervention activities that you can use right away, ideas for introducing and using AAC at home, and ideas for adapting classic therapy activities for nonspeaking learners.

4. So many words, so little space - the lament of those who design AAC systems for their students. Learn how to manage your AAC system space effectively by using core and fringe vocabulary strategies.

5. Take home templates for communication you can use right now: You will be given sample planning and intervening forms that you can begin to use right away.

6. Learn some simple strategies for alternative access: Students with motor impairments and motor planning issues pose particular challenges for accessing communication systems and academic materials. Partner Assisted Scanning is an effective way to bring dynamic display to all students. NOTE: How to teach switch use,

electronic scanning, or eye gaze is not within the scope of this book.

7. Learn strategies for adapting AAC materials for students with cortical vision issues: Acquire a toolkit of strategies for working with this difficult population. Cortical vision impairment is not about visual acuity; it is a different and ever-changing phenomenon. There are some simple strategies you can use to enhance these students' access to AAC.

8. Use what you already know as a SLP or parent to teach your students/child who use/s AAC: Many strategies for teaching language apply to all students with communication needs. Learn how to apply what you already know about teaching and learning strategies for language, as well as acquiring new skill sets to apply. Learn how to carry over these strategies to home activities so you can communicate with your child.

CHAPTER 1
Introduction to Terminology & AAC

What is Communication?

"The single biggest problem in communication is the illusion that it has taken place."

— George Bernard Shaw

Speech-language pathologists tend to focus on the development of speech and language skills, while sometimes forgetting to focus on their ultimate purpose: **to communicate.**

So, what is communication?

The National Joint Committee for the Communicative Needs of Persons with Severe Disabilities defines communication as, "Any act by which one person gives to or receives from another person information about that person's needs, desires, perceptions, knowledge, or affective states. Communication may be intentional or unintentional, may involve conventional or unconventional signals, may take linguistic or nonlinguistic forms, and may occur through spoken or other modes."

Note that the focus in this definition is on the shared meaning between communication partners. It is not on speech, or even on language, but on interaction.

Note too, that per this definition, unintentional behaviors and nonlinguistic forms can signal communication.

Communication, then, can more simply be defined as the process of exchanging ideas and information; involving the encoding, or formulation, of ideas and the decoding, or processing of them.

In order for communication to happen, the partners involved need to:

> be aware of the cause-effect relationships between one's behavior and the other's

> have something to communicate or exchange

Language, on the other hand, is a code that has been developed in a culture that uses specific symbols that have arbitrarily been determined to mean something. (A symbol stands for something else, with no apparent prior relationship). Language competence is required for communicative competence.

What is Augmentative-Alternative Communication?

According to the American Speech–Language–Hearing Association (ASHA), it is, "…a set of procedures and processes by which an individual's communication skills (i.e. production as well as comprehension) can be maximized for functional and effective communication. It involves supplementing or replacing natural speech… with aided… and/or unaided symbols…"

Note that this definition:

> refers to communication approaches that augment speech or serve as an alternative.

refers to all methods that make communication easier or possible.

may include facial expressions; gestures; an alphabet, words or picture board; a computer; and other similar systems.

The ASHA AAC Glossary defines communication as "...based on the use of individual words of our language. True communication is spontaneous and novel. Therefore, communication systems cannot be based significantly on pre-stored sentences. Communication requires access to vocabulary of individual words suitable to our needs that are multiple and subject to change. These words must be selected to form the sentences that we wish to say."

According to ASHA, too, the "goal of augmentative and alternative communication use is the most effective interaction possible. Anything less represents a compromise of the individual's human potential."

It needs to be the goal of AAC intervention to provide our clients, children, and students with the words to say whatever they want to, whenever they want to, wherever they want to.

I recently had an exchange with a SLP new to learning about AAC. She was asking my opinion about the materials she had been using and what she should be doing. She was discouraged when I said a 20-location static display device wasn't a sufficient communication system, really, for her students to be communicating with. I said I'd prefer a paper- based system that is robust over a SGD that is not.

It is simply a matter of "real estate."

If a light tech device only has 20 buttons and 1 of them says "I want an apple," how does the child say, "I hate apples." "I don't want an apple." "Johnny took my apple." "This apple is yucky." "I like green apples better than red ones." "I lost my apple." "The apple fell on the floor." There is simply not enough room on that 20-symbol display. And if you're focusing on core words, there is no room for fringe.

With 20 locations for messages or words, the child does not have even the 25 core words that toddlers use the most.

The same limitations exist when you use an app that offers only 2 or 4 or 6 choices.

We'll say more about this later.

Terminology: What is AAC?

There are some terms that will reoccur throughout discussions of AAC. They are briefly defined here and will be discussed in more depth throughout this book. While a Glossary would normally be at the back of the book, it is too important for the stakeholders to understand the terminology, as it will be used throughout the process.

AAC System

A group of strategies, aids, symbols, and component pieces that work together to allow an individual to communicate; supplementing any body language, spoken or written language skills.

Access

The way in which the individual makes a selection of a word or message on the AAC system.

- Direct selection access involves the user pointing or touching the system directly.

- Scanning involves using a switch to activate the system's movement through the messages available in sequential order until the user activates the switch again (or a second switch) to make a selection.

- Eye gaze is an access mode for those with significant motor disabilities wherein a built-in camera tracks the eye movements of the individual, allowing the user to point to the message button with their eyes. Eye gaze is faster and more efficient than using a scanning system.

Aided Communication

An AAC system that utilizes something that is external to the user; such as a communication book or device. (In contrast, speech, vocalization, gestures, and signs are examples of Unaided communication).

Aided Language Stimulation (AlgS)

A strategy in which a communication partner teaches the AAC user the meanings of symbols, their locations, and how/when to use them through modeling their use while providing verbal input for genuine communication interactions.

Alternative

Instead of speech; replacing speech.

Assistive Technology

This is an umbrella term used to talk about assistive and adaptive devices or systems for individuals with disabilities. It includes any piece of equipment or software program or app that can be used to increase the functional abilities of students with disabilities. This umbrella includes AAC.

Augmented

In addition to the user's speech to supplement and/ or provide support and additional communication.

Apps

There are numerous AAC apps available for your iOS devices. We will discuss them further later. But know that there are many, many apps available for AAC, but relatively very few that are robust enough to be considered appropriate AAC systems.

Books and Boards

Over the years there have been any number of configurations for communication boards or books. We will talk more about these when we talk about the components of an AAC system. For quick reference; know that core word boards with fringe vocabulary flip strips and PODD communication books are your best bet.

Cell

An area on the communication system that contains the information for a message or part of a message.

Communication Breakdown and Repair

Breakdown refers to a failure to communicate in an interaction.

Repair refers to a strategy that fixes that breakdown; a compensatory strategy that fixes those interactions where 1 or both partners are confused or misunderstood.

Communicative Competence

Functional communication within the individual's environment that allows the individual to meet his communication needs

Complex Communication Need (CCN)

Usually used to refer to those AAC learners who have significant disabilities and needs beyond simply replacing their speech. These AAC users have a combination of physical, sensory, and other challenges that make communication difficult.

Contextual and Context-Dependent

Communication can be limited to within specific situations or topics; the child may not be able to communicate without the context's clues

Core Vocabulary

Those high frequency words which we use the most often. These words are usually useable in a variety of contexts on a variety of topics, and can be combined together in a large number of ways to create novel messages. A variety of parts of speech are represented in core words, but rarely nouns. About 80% of what we say is comprised of core words. There are many core word lists of various sizes. Most researchers include about 350 core words as the base for much of what we say.

Cues

These can be visual, tactile, auditory, or other sensory information that helps the AAC user understand what is happening.

Decontextualized

Communication or practice which occurs outside of the context in which the individual would use the communication responses.

Dedicated System

An AAC device (including an iPad) whose function is restricted to only communication.

Direct Access

Refers to the user's selecting vocabulary by pointing, depressing, activating a cell directly.

Dynamic Display

Refers to a system that has navigation conventions that allow the user to move from page to page in a systematic fashion.

Emergent Literacy

The early stages of literacy skills development; such as orientation of the book, acknowledgement of the relationship of print to speech.

Expressive Language

How the individual uses communication; speech, pictures, text.

Eye Gaze

Refers to a system in which the individual uses their eyes to make a selection or activate a cell on a device.

Fitzgerald Key

The left to right organization of vocabulary in the system, so that the user constructs a message moving from persons to actions to descriptors and nouns.

Fringe Vocabulary

Those topic specific words that are used less often and are less useful in a variety of contexts; they are usually nouns, and make up only about 20% of the words one would find in a 100-word sample.

Gesture

A general term for movements that are made with hands, arms, and facial expressions.

Signs are more conventional gestures that have been ascribed meaning by a group of users and become a part of the lexicon (which is, essentially, a catalogue of a language's words)

Head Mouse

A head-controlled mouse that acts exactly like a desktop mouse on any computer or tablet for individuals who cannot use their hands.

Head Tracker

A wireless optical sensor that tracks a tiny reflective target places on the user's forehead, cap, or glasses frame. Movement of the student's head acts controls the "mouse" of the computer.

Head Pointer

A pointing object (a stick of some sort) that attaches to the individual's head so that he can select items on the AAC system without use of his hands.

Low Tech

An AAC system that is paper-based; such as bards and books or uses minimal technology; such as a single message switch or a small device with limited message capacity.

Nonspeaking Communication

This one is a little tricky. We tend to equate nonverbal and nonspeaking. However, this is not the case. Nonspeaking communication refers to communication that does not use words in any form; including written or pictorial or signed. Rather, it is communication via body language, facial expression, and gesture.

Partner Assisted Scanning (PAS)

A no-technology strategy in which the communication partner scans through the choices available on the (no/low-tech) AAC system, always in the same order, looking for an agreed-upon response from the individual to accept an option. Partners present the choices in the same sequential order every time. This strategy is usually used with an individual with significant motor or visual problems who has difficulty accessing an AAC system independently.

The human partner is called a "smart partner" in contrast to computer assisted scanning because the computer cannot adapt to the individual's day to day or minute to minute fluctuations or read facial expressions and body language the way a live partner can.

PECS

Picture Exchange Communication System is a system originally designed to establish communicative intent in children with Autism who had no intentional communication. Initially 2 partners are needed; one to provide support needed to have the child hand the other a symbol to exchange for what he is asking for.

Initial stages are limited to requesting, and in my experience many students lose interest in the system when it becomes laborious to scan through the choices to find what they want, when the symbols are Velcro'd to different places each time they are used.

PECS does NOT refer to a specific group of pictures (see below), but to the specific ABA-based system.

PCS

Picture Communication Symbols refer to the Mayer-Johnson's line of picture symbols; currently provided in Boardmaker software or on-line subscription. These symbols are not equivalent to PECS, and should not be referred to this way.

Another symbol system - Symbol Stix - is currently used in most AAC systems and apps. Yet a third symbol set is making inroads in AAC; Smarty Symbols (which you will see in this book) are designed by the Smarty Ears app people.

Receptive Language

Comprehension of language; understanding of words, pictures, or signs.

Scaffolding

The partner adjusts the environment, the structure, the cues, the input in some way that allows the user to participate

Scanning

A presentation of choices one at a time or one group at a time, where the user signals acceptance of a choice with a pre-determined response (eye blink, blink, etc).

Auditory Scanning - the choices are presented verbally

Visual Scanning - the choices are presented visually

Auditory-Visual - the choices are presented both auditors and visually.

SGD (speech generating device) or VOCA (voice output communication assistant)

Voice output can be either digital (recorded speech) or synthesized (computer generated) speech.

High-tech devices are referred to as SGDs because the speech can be computer generated. However, many high-tech devices also have the capability of using digitized speech in some instances. These devices use dynamic display; where there are multiple pages of symbols which link together, allowing the individual to refine and categorize their vocabulary.

Low tech static display devices use recorded speech only to provide the voice output. These devices have static displays, where a single overlay is provided and requires a partner to change that display/overlay in order to access more or different vocabulary.

Static Display

A device or system that has a single page available at any one time. This type of system requires that the user or a communication partner changes the picture/word overlay to change topics or refine vocabulary needed.

Switch

An electronic piece that connects to the AAC system and allows the user to push/activate the switch when the desired choice is spoken.

Symbol/word choices are spoken or highlighted on the device one at a time, or one group at a time. The user activates the switch when their choice is presented.

Switches can be activated by a variety of different mechanisms; including, but not limited to, eye blink, depression by a body part, joystick press or pull, use of oral pressure, and even movement in the area of the button.

Symbol

Something that represents or stands for something else. In the simplest form, a symbol is a signal that is interpreted the same way by at least two people.

There are 2 types of visual symbols; graphic and lexical. Graphic symbols include line drawings, photographs, color or black & white images. Lexical symbols are letters or words.

Symbol Transparency and Opacity

AAC systems can use concrete objects, photographs, life-like drawings, or line drawing symbols. Symbols are said to be transparent when what they represent is obvious to any communication partner either immediately or with an initial explanation. Opacity refers to symbols that are abstract, don't have any resemblance to the word or concept, and which are not easily identified without the accompanying label or direct instruction.

Text-to-speech

When the user types a word that the device speaks.

Verbal Referencing

A scaffolding strategy whereby the communication partner either speaks about what the child is doing or what he/she is doing as a model of the kind of 'thinking through the process' that the child should do while figuring out where to go on the AAC system. The first instance helps children who do not know where their bodies are in space or have difficulty controlling their bodies. The use of verbally referencing as they model is recommended for use with all children, to "outline" the process needed to generate a message. (Porter, G. 2007)

Voice Output Communication Aid

A device that speaks for the individual.

Word Prediction

Software that provides assistance when the user is using the keyboard to construct a message. The device provides choices of whole words as the user begins to spell; predicting what the word might be and providing a number of choices, to minimize the keystrokes necessary for the user to construct his message.

CHAPTER 2

Myths and Misconceptions

T he myths of AAC are a combination of misconceptions and misinformation. Unfortunately, they are both pervasive and dangerous. They may continue to be perpetuated by beliefs that communication must be verbal. Here are some myths:

That AAC is restricted to specific options.

That use of AAC will prevent children from developing speech.

That there are prerequisite skills that must be developed before an individual is able to use AAC.

That AAC systems are too complex for individuals with intellectual disabilities.

That the child is too young to use AAC.

That AAC is only for someone who has no speech at all.

That AAC is a last resort.

However, AAC is necessary because:

Individuals who lack an appropriate communication mode may use inappropriate behaviors to communicate.

Individuals who have given up in their attempts to participate become passive.

There is no evidence that use of an AAC system inhibits acquisition of verbal language skills and there is evidence that use of AAC enhances verbal language skills, participation in academic and social activities, and quality of life. and - most importantly - everyone deserves to have a voice.

Not too long ago I got a call from a mother. She was interested in looking into AAC for her child, but the school district said the child was too young. How old was he? He was 6.

A week later I had the same experience. This time, however, the child was 3. As soon as I put a dynamic display device in front of her with core words to use in our play interactions she began to use the system independently to direct my actions and her choice of activities, including which colors of markers she wanted.

Too soon for AAC?

A few years ago, I attended an IEP meeting for a girl for whom I was providing consultation. The school district was appalled when I suggested an AAC system as a repair strategy. She was verbal; but with a repertoire of less than 3 dozen words. Their response; "We're not giving up on speech. It's too soon!" How old was she? She was 9!

And note that I suggested an AAC system as a repair strategy, not as a replacement for speech. I wanted her to have a way to communicate when she did not have the words in her repertoire.

BUSTING THE MYTHS: Too young for AAC?

Some parents and professionals believe that AAC is a last resort for their nonspeaking or minimally verbal children, and should only be used when there is no more hope for developing speech.

Unfortunately, this all too often means that children (and some adults) have no means of communicating for far too long; resulting in frustration, negative behaviors, and significant limitations on their language development, access to curriculum in school, access to social interactions at home and in the community, and in adapted living skills.

Waiting too long to provide a mode of communication denies the child the opportunity to learn language, acquire vocabulary, and express himself appropriately. Waiting too long to provide an appropriate mode too often means communicating with an inappropriate mode. Research shows that any intervention delayed beyond a child's first three years has less significant impact, and that children - including those with disabilities - learn faster and more easily when they are young. Lack of access to communication results in the individual being excluded from appropriate educational and vocational placements, restricting social development and quality of life.

Rather than being a last resort, AAC can serve as an important tool for language development and should be implemented as a preventative strategy - before communication failure occurs. Romski and Sevcik (2005) conclude that young children with complex communication needs (CCN) should receive services early in their development to augment natural speech and support development of language and communication. Withholding AAC intervention not only impacts building language skills, but also has an impact upon cognitive, play, social, and literacy skills development.

From birth babies communicate to us. We recognize these communicative behaviors and respond to them; reinforcing them and expanding upon them. We do not wait until they can speak to us to recognize and build on their communications. We do not wait until they can communicate independently to provide scaffolding for building more communication skills. Rather we interpret what they are doing to communicate and model additional possibilities. We work on building both nonspeaking and verbal skills simultaneously. Similarly, we can work on AAC skills and speech simultaneously.

BUSTING THE MYTHS: Use of AAC will prevent the child from speaking.

Parents and professionals may also believe that use of AAC will stifle the child's potential verbal skills and/or serve as a "crutch" upon which the child will become reliant. However, research has shown that use of AAC often stimulates verbal skills in users with the potential to be at least partially verbal.

Children need access to appropriate and effective modes of communication as soon as possible. Without an appropriate way to communicate genuine messages, individuals frequently use inappropriate behaviors to communicate, or withdraw. Struggling to learn to speak, while having no other way to communicate, leads usually to frustration.

Further, those who have access to AAC tend to increase their verbal skills. So, not only is there no evidence to suggest that AAC use hinders speech development, there is evidence that suggests access to AAC has a positive impact on speech development. AAC is now cited as evidence-based practice for facilitating speech in nonspeaking children.

Why AAC use promotes speech development is not precisely known. Theories include the possibility that use of AAC reduces the physical and social/emotional demands of speech and that the symbols/words provided visually serve as consistent cues and the speech output provides consistent models. Although the goal of AAC intervention is not necessarily to promote speech production, the effect appears to be that it is a result.

BUSTING THE MYTHS: There are no prerequisite skills needed!

Many times, parents are told children need to have a set of prerequisite skills in order to qualify for or benefit from AAC - particularly high-tech

AAC - and that their young and/or severely disabled children (and adults) do not yet possess those skills.

In addition, some professionals believe that there is a hierarchy of AAC systems that each individual needs to move through; utilizing no- or low-technology strategies before gaining access to high-technology systems.

In fact, this outlook only tends to limit the type of supports provided and limit the extent to which language may be developed.

First, there are NO prerequisites for communication; everyone does it, including infants. And as we've seen above, all children learn to communicate before learning to speak.

Second, research does not support the idea of a hierarchy of AAC systems, and shows that very young children can learn to use signs and symbols before they learn to talk. Research has also shown that very young children with complex communication needs have learned to use abstract symbols, photographs, and voice output devices during play and reading activities.

In fact, requiring an individual to learn multiple symbol systems or AAC systems as they develop skills merely serves to make learning to communicate more difficult.

One of the things we have learned about teaching individuals to use AAC systems is that the stability of vocabulary is important. Being able to locate the words in the same location every time they use the system significantly lightens the cognitive load of looking for the words wanted or needed for a message. The less cognitive attention that needs to be paid to finding vocabulary the more available for formulating the message. When we make the user move through a hierarchy of devices, we constantly present them with different arrangements of words; making it more difficult for them to learn.

Voice output is more like the natural give and take of spoken communication interactions. Providing access to voice output provides a speech model for users and provides clear intent to communication partners. Voice output provides auditory feedback while students are learning symbol meaning - unlike no-technology systems. Voice output allows the user to gain attention even when partners are not paying attention directly to them and allows for interactions with partners who are less familiar with their communication modes and strategies. Voice output also allows a user to repair a breakdown in communication when they have not been understood.

Use of a high-technology system with voice output provides an interaction that is most like natural verbal speech. An environment is provided in which is it easier to learn to interact. Providing access to the symbols early on, accompanied by voice output, provides models in addition to those (hopefully) being provided by Aided Language Stimulation, which we will discuss shortly.

BUSTING THE MYTHS: But he has some speech!

Many parents and professionals believe that AAC is only for individuals who are completely nonspeaking. Students who have some speech skills are frequently not provided access to AAC systems in the belief that intervention should focus only on building their speaking skills.

However, if speech is not functional to meet **all** of the individual's communication needs - that is, if the student does not have sufficient vocabulary, is not understood in all environments, or if speech is only echolalic or perseverative - AAC should be considered.

"Any child whose speech is not effective to meet all communication needs or who does not have speech is a candidate for AAC. Any child whose language comprehension skills are being claimed to be 'insufficient to warrant' AAC training is a candidate for Aided Language Stimulation and AAC." (Porter, G).

The individual who says a few words or phrases needs to increase his vocabulary and communication functions.

The individual whose family and care staff can understand him may not be understood by others in the community.

The individual who can repeat everything he hears - is echolalic - does not necessarily use these utterances appropriately and still cannot interact in a social, academic, or daily living exchange.

The individual who perseverates on a given utterance usually lacks the ability to formulate new utterances in the face of desiring to communicate. Once he has his partner's attention, how does he communicate what it is he really wants to say but cannot?

None of these individuals has functional speech to meet all of their communication needs. All are potential candidates for AAC.

BUSTING THE MYTHS: She's not smart enough for AAC.

When working with individuals with severe disabilities - particularly intellectual disabilities - many professionals assume the individual is too cognitively impaired to use AAC.

Kangas and Lloyd (1988) wrote, "that there is no 'sufficient data to support the view' that these individuals cannot benefit from AAC because they have difficulty paying attention, understanding cause and effect, don't appear to want to communicate, are unable to acquire skills that demonstrate comprehension of language, are too intellectually impaired."

Unfortunately, there continues to be this misconception, and professionals continue to posit arbitrary skills that individuals must attain before providing AAC intervention.

All too often professionals - and even family - underestimate the potential abilities of these individuals. We must proceed with the notion of the "least dangerous assumption." That is, we must proceed with the plan that, if we are incorrect, will cause the least damage to the individual. In fact, ASHA has a strong stance against "Cognitive Referencing," the practice of restricting services based on the perceived limitations of the individual's cognitive skills.

"Cognitive Referencing is the practice of comparing IQ scores and language scores as a factor for determining eligibility for speech-language intervention. It is based on the assumption that language functioning cannot surpass cognitive levels. However, according to research, some language abilities may in fact surpass cognitive levels. Therefore, ASHA does not support the use of cognitive referencing." (ASHA, 2016)

Unfortunately, the discrepancy model does not take into account the fact that cognitive and language skills are intertwined and interdependent; not linear. Language is as likely to improve cognitive function as increased cognitive skills are to improve language. (Nelson, N. 1995, Deak, 2014)

ASHA's position statement concludes:

"Evidence from research has shown that all individuals can benefit from appropriate communication services to improve the effectiveness of their communication. A child's cognitive age relates to where along the continuum of communication he or she will begin the communication and language process. A child's cognitive age should not be used to deny communication services and supports.

The use of "discrepancy" between measured cognitive and measured language levels is not an acceptable approach to eligibility decisions. It is appropriate to provide communication services to an individual whose language age is commensurate with his or her mental age.

The relationship between language and cognition is neither simple nor static. Research has shown that individuals with disabilities whose cognitive and language skills were measured as equal nonetheless benefit from language intervention."

Believing the individual can acquire communication skills, we proceed with a plan to provide an AAC system and intervention. There can be no damage from providing someone with a way to communicate.

If we believe the individual cannot acquire these skills and thus do not provide an AAC system or intervention, we have done immense damage if we are wrong. Poor performance is more often related to the competence of the intervention, not of the individual.

Research and observation continue to indicate that there is no benefit to denying access to AAC to individuals with significant disabilities. Intervention should be based on the idea that learning is based on the strengthening of neural connections through experiences and that repetition of these connections through multiple modes facilitates learning. Providing users with rich experiences with their AAC systems builds on the neural patterns and facilitates communication skills building. Not providing AAC services based on preconceived ideas about the cognitive skills of the individuals, simply continues to segregate and limit access to life experiences for them.

Nickola Wolf Nelson suggests we ask, not who can benefit from intervention based on their IQ, but, "Who has language and communication skills that are insufficient to support them in the important contexts of their lives?" She cites the evidence from Lahey (1992), Cole (1990, 1992), & Terrell (1978) that:

1. Cognitive and language tests may reflect the same things;

2. Some combinations of language tests and cognitive tests show a discrepancy when others may not—and at some- times, but not at others;

3. Formal testing often yields biased results for children from diverse cultural and linguistic communities;

4. Formal tests fail to assess contextually-based needs for language intervention;

5. Validity for determining the need for language intervention services is questionable; and,

6. Children can benefit from language intervention services whether or not they show discrepancies

Students should be served based on their unmet communication needs. Communication is a basic need and a basic right, says the National Joint Committee for Communication Needs of Persons with Severe Disabilities (1992).

BUSTING THE MYTHS: PECS is good enough.

Many school districts also subscribe to the idea (some call it a myth) that the PECS is sufficiently robust. The Picture Exchange Communication System (PECS) is widely used in school districts as the AAC system provided to students. It is good at establishing communicative intent in a child who does not appear to demonstrate this. In fact, it originated as a way to teach children with autism how to initiate communication by approaching others.

PECS books use Velcro to move symbols between their pages and the cover sentence strip. Use of Velcro means a lack of stability; pictures can be in a different location every time the child opens the book. Too much cognitive energy can be consumed by trying to find the picture wanted.

Learning through motor planning, which research has shown to be effective for some is obviated by use of Velcro and random vocabulary positions (think about getting into a rental car whose brake pedal is in a different place). Effective AAC users pay little attention to the symbol; rather they rely upon location and motor patterns to find vocabulary. Instability of vocabulary location can eventually lead to frustration. And the increased effort needed to use PECS will often lead to the child abandoning it.

PECS books have limited vocabulary. I once encountered a young girl who was small and slight. She had a PECS book that was a large 3-ring binder with many pages full of Velcro'd pictures. It was almost as heavy as she was. It required someone else to carry it around for her. It was an effort for her to find the word she wanted at each communicative attempt. And while teachers, SLPs and parents continued to add vocabulary to it, most of the vocabulary available was nouns. How was she expected to expand her language skills without the building blocks of syntax? Where were the adjectives (other than colors) to elaborate? Where were morphology and syntax? Once I provided a system that allowed - and assisted - her in constructing sentences, she was able to communicate much more effectively. Inappropriate behaviors decreased.

BUSTING THE MYTHS: He has an iPad. He should pick it up and use it!

Unfortunately, there are also those who believe that simply providing access to an AAC system will solve the communication problems of the user.

The AAC system cannot "fix" the individual or their communication difficulties. While use of AAC will facilitate development of speech or language, and of literacy skills, and will increase the individuals' ability to communicate effectively, it will not do so simply by being there.

The AAC system is a tool and, like any tool, the user needs to know how to use it. And for most of those individuals, direct, specific, and structured intervention and opportunities need to be provided.

The success of the AAC system is not dependent upon only the individual's skills and cognitive abilities. It is also not only dependent upon the completeness or robustness of the AAC system. It is strongly dependent upon the willingness, training, and responsiveness of partners. Partners who do not understand the need for the AAC system are less likely to respond to the individual's communication attempt with it. If the partners have low expectations of the AAC learner, do not respond consistently, do not use aided input consistently or do not provide sufficient communication opportunities the AAC learner is not likely to progress. Communication partners have a significant responsibility.

Who Should Use AAC and Why?

People who use AAC are those individuals whose current mode of communication does not meet all their communication needs; restricts the quality and quantity of interactions with others.

All individuals are considered potential candidates for AAC; ASHA and the Joint Commission for Persons with Disabilities have a "zero exclusion" criterion and consider not whether an individual is eligible for services, but rather consider where along the continuum they are currently operating as a starting point. As long as there is a discrepancy between needs and abilities, an individual qualifies for services in AAC.

Best practices also dictate that, while there is a relationship between cognitive and linguistic skills, this is not a causal relationship. Language skills are just as likely to affect cognition as vice versa.

There is no such thing as the typical or average AAC user. You will find individuals who need access to AAC from all age groups and a wide range of diagnostic categories. There is almost no group of clients or students you will work with, where you will not find some need for AAC.

Children who do not have speech or whose speech is not meeting their communication needs need to be considered as candidates for AAC intervention. Among children, cerebral palsy, Autism Spectrum Disorder and other developmental disabilities probably are the largest groups of AAC users; however, there are a variety of other disabilities or disorders that will require you to think about AAC access. Children with Angelman's Syndrome, girls with Rett syndrome, developmental apraxia of speech and a host of less common or low-incidence disorders can show up on the SLP's caseload.

Not all of these users require high-technology AAC systems to communicate. But they do require a robust system that allows them to be effective communicators. The "...ultimate goal of an AAC intervention is not to find a technological solution to the communication problem, but to enable the individual to efficiently and effectively engage in a variety of interactions." (Beukelman and Mirenda, 1998)

They all also require that there be partners who keep them motivated and stimulated, who provide opportunities for them to communicate, who assess their AAC systems on an on-going bases, and who provided the aided input and modeling needed for them to learn how to use their AAC system and language. These partners also need to know the wide range of communication functions that need to be represented in the users' toolbox.

As we continue to talk about AAC systems, bear in mind that a functional AAC system is a compilation of strategies and pieces that allow the individual to communicate effectively a variety of intents in a variety of contexts, with a variety of partners.

All of us use a variety of modes to communicate. Different modes are useful in different contexts. I cringe when a user has pointed to the item in front of him or used a single word response, in response to the question, "What do you want?" and the adult demands he used his AAC system to construct a complete sentence. All of us use gestures and single word responses quite often. This is important to remember in intervention. The level of language used should fit the communication event.

Also bear in mind that communication needs a purpose - an intent. The individual must have something that he wishes to communicate - impart - to someone else. It is important to make situations motivating and meaningful in order to create an environment in which an individual who is just learning to communicate has something he wants to say and the means to say it. Sometimes we just need to look a little further to find what really motivates this individual to want to communicate.

A case in point: I was called in to consult a district regarding a boy of 10 with autism. He had been using a PECS (Picture Exchange Communication System) board with symbols for favorite foods and activities. Pictures were also used during specific activities in the class. These Velcro'd pictures were only available during the specific activity, and were limited to symbols required for that activity. They were also limited to nouns, with a few activity-associated verbs.

Staff told me he had been successful for a while with pictures, and was great at using them to request food (he was always hungry), but wasn't using them for other activities and so they did not think he was "ready" for a more complex system.

When I observed in his classroom, I saw him first during an art activity where he was required to cut and paste, then color. This was a boy who had poor fine motor skills and did not like or ever **want** to do cutting and coloring. But the symbols for the activity required to him say that he wanted scissors, he wanted glue, he wanted the red crayon, etc. He most clearly did **not** want any of these things – and "Not" was not available among the symbols.

Given an activity he enjoyed and appropriate symbols to use, he was clearly able to use them. His vocabulary was limited, as he had always been restricted to a noun-based vocabulary, but he clearly knew what the pictures were for and how to use them.

Lessons learned:

1. Verbal communicators are able to tell you when they don't want something or don't want to say what you want them to. Nonspeaking communicators have the same right to say "I don't want to" as everyone else.

2. Only giving the individual the words to say specific, limited messages does not give them the ability to communicate.

3. As Gayle Porter says, "…a child who uses speech will independently select the words she wishes from the vast array she hears/uses every day. A child who uses AAC will independently select the words she wishes to use from the vocabulary other people have chosen to model and, for aided symbols, made available for her to use." (Porter & Kirkland) And a child who uses a limited AAC system will sometimes NOT choose to select words that do not say what he wants them to.

Best practices also dictate that, while there is a relationship between cognitive and linguistic skills, this is not a causal relationship. Language skills are just as likely to affect cognition as vice versa.

CHAPTER 3

A Robust AAC System: What Do We Mean? And Why is it Important

" A child who uses speech will independently select the words she wishes from the vast vocabulary she hears/uses every day. A child who uses AAC will independently select the words she wishes to use from the vocabulary other people have chosen to model and, for aided symbols, made available for her to use." (Porter & Kirkland). This cannot be overstated. We cannot learn if the student can use more vocabulary if we don't give it to her and teach it to her.

A functional AAC system is a compilation of strategies that allow the individual to communicate effectively a variety of intents in a variety of contexts, with a variety of partners. We need to recognize that the different modes of communication are useful and necessary in different contexts while also remembering that we need to provide users with sufficient vocabulary - in whatever mode - to allow them to communicate genuine messages.

I know a woman who has a very robust and diverse AAC system. She has Cerebral Palsy and uses a wheelchair. Mounted on her wheelchair is a high-tech dynamic display speech generating device (SGD). She is able to access the touch screen with her thumb. Also attached to the arm of her wheelchair are a notebook containing words and phrases that she uses most often and an alphabet page which she uses with her most familiar communication partners to tell the first letter of each word she wants to say.

In terms of fostering the most "robust" AAC system, it is important to teach flexibility and have alternative means available for when the primary mode of communication is not practical at that time or is unavailable for whatever reason; if the high-tech device is broken or malfunctioning, or has lost its battery charge, for example.

In addition, students might need to be able to use different communication modes in different social contexts. For example, what might be appropriate with friends in an informal interaction would be out of place when interacting with a teacher, or in a formal situation with adults. Similarly, a student who communicates with his classroom aides with signs would need to have the flexibility to communicate via a different mode in the community with individuals who do not understand signs.

We all use a variety of modes of communication; the mode at any given instance being reliant on context and intent. The same should be true of our nonverbal (non-speaking) clients, students, children. In fact, use of multiple component systems has been shown to be more effective and more natural (Erickson).

Any system must provide well organized language, a wide variety of vocabulary, and stability of vocabulary and its location. So, when asked the question, "Does this individual need a low technology system or a high-technology device?" The answer is, "Yes. All of the above." At all times we should remember to focus on the individual and their communication; NOT the technology.

There are 3 basic types of AAC system components; no technology, low technology, and high-technology. And there are 3 basic arrangements of vocabulary within those systems; core vocabulary, topical vocabulary, and pragmatically organized vocabulary.

We are going to start with talking about vocabulary organization. Access to the words with which to communicate is important, and navigation - the movement from one page or display of symbols to another

- becomes key in that access. Once the vocabulary exceeds the number of cells or spaces on a single page, the user needs to navigate through pages to find the vocabulary he wants to use

Sometimes the need for navigation causes the user to lose his place, to forget what word he was looking for, or to lose track of the message he was constructing. The user also needs to remember the steps needed to get to a specific page or word. The cognitive load increases with the need to navigate to find and access words. For students with motor impairments, this can also increase the load significantly. Now the user has to focus on two difficult tasks; language production and motor movement.

Choosing the words to put into the system is another important consideration. Which words will the user need? And once the list of words is generated, there comes the question of how to get them all into the AAC system? Robin Parker (PrAACticalAAC.org) once suggested that a way to conceptualize the difficulty with this is to write down all of the words the individual might need onto three-by-five cards. Pull out the words that should always be immediately available. Sort the rest into categories. Then note the size of the piles of cards. Some piles might be too big to put onto one page, so now those need to be sorted into smaller related piles. Sometimes a few words don't seem to go with any particular pile. Sometimes, there are words that could go with more than one pile.

Once the category piles are made, see if the number of piles matches the number of buttons allocated for that specific user's page. Are there too many? Now what? You might need to combine some categories. That might mean further subcategories. There needs to be consideration of both the number of buttons per page and the number of pages in the system.

Once you start putting these words into a system, you have to consider how they will be arranged on the page. Moving from left to right mimics reading and is a good way to go. But, if you have a motorically impaired user who can't reach to one side of the other, placing high frequency words on the easier-to-access side makes more sense. The words should be placed in the system in a meaningful arrangement. Consider what is meaningful and useful for the individual. Once the pages have been made, remember that vocabulary should not be moved around.

Clearly, the concept of vocabulary organization is complicated, but it doesn't always need to be. AAC users tell us that the most important concepts for them in AAC use are the ability to say exactly what they want to say; and say it as quickly as possible (AAC Institute, 2009). The ability to do this is dependent upon the way in which language is represented in the AAC system.

In any AAC system, we need to have sufficient vocabulary for the student to communicate anything he wants. One of the factors that makes an AAC system robust is the use and organization of vocabulary; specifically, core vocabulary along with a healthy dose of fringe.

As I've said, use of pre-programed phrases and sentences for many responses has been shown to be ineffective. You must allow for genuine message construction and you need vocabulary for a variety of functions. AAC users who are competent communicators tell us that pre-programed phrases rarely, if ever, meet their needs. The most notable exception to this is social interaction and comment phrases.

Research tells us that there are two types of vocabulary: core and fringe. (Baker, 2012) Core vocabulary is identified as the most commonly used words in a language. They are reusable words that can fit many interactions. They are consistent across demographics. Core vocabulary mostly consists of pronouns, prepositions, determiners, verbs, adjectives, and conjunctions. These words are considered the building blocks of language. With them, you can build an unlimited number of phrases and sentences. Core vocabulary is comprised of high frequency words that are multi-purpose and versatile and is independent of cognitive ability. Between 350 and 500 words compromise core for most adults.

Fringe vocabulary contains words that are used infrequently and are not flexible or versatile. Where core words are a small number of words that are applicable across place and topic, fringe vocabulary contains a large number of words with less applicability. Core words are used frequently while fringe words are used less frequently. Core words are used in multiple contexts and environments; fringe words are less applicable and may be used only in some contexts. Core vocabulary includes a variety of parts of speech, where fringe vocabulary contains largely nouns.

Approximately 80% of words used in a language sample of 100 words will be core words. Since many of the core words will have been repeated, there will actually have been a small number of words used. Only 20% of words used in the 100-word sample will be fringe words. The number of different fringe words used will be larger, since fringe words are not repeated as often as core words. Fringe words are relevant to a specific topic and may be very important to a specific user. If we're talking about access to academic vocabulary, Tier 1 and some Tier 2 words will be core. Tier 3 words will be largely fringe.

Based on this research, many see the function of the AAC vocabulary as providing a small set of consistent and predictable words that occur often and comprise 80% of spoken messages. Core words provide the basic structure of our messages, where fringe words provide individualized details. The AAC user is able to say many things with a core vocabulary, but may be limited to single word responses with only fringe words. Core vocabulary AAC organization provides an organized vocabulary set that users can use across environments and contexts and that intervention can target in any context.

While we're building vocabulary comprehension and use, we also need to build the variety of functions the child uses. Rather than only focusing on wants and needs (requesting: want that, put here, read it), we should also be modeling and targeting greetings/partings (hi, go away); requests for not just objects but also for assistance: (help me, you help) information: (who that?, what that?, where she?) recurrence: (more, again); existence: (that, here) possession: (mine, your, that mine) nonexistence: (no, none) disappearance: (gone) rejection: (don't) cessation: (stop) comment/describe: (bad, funny, big;) directing agent and events: (get) name, associate. Teaching becomes focused on critical thinking and critical concepts; rather than on words that will not be used again.

Two alternative systems of organizing vocabulary in communication books that have been developed have gained more widespread use recently. Each is developed with a slightly different philosophy of augmented communication. These appear to be the two best-known/most often used organization of communication books that provide sufficient vocabulary to meet a student's communication needs; and whose implementation procedures provide a structured format to teach AAC. Other organizational systems still exist, but for the most part have been subsumed into these two.

Core vocabulary boards, books, and devices focus on providing students with those words that research has shown to be the most used to generate language responses. Core word teaching serves as a great method for teaching language; particularly generative language teaching, in that all parts of speech are represented. Core word-based systems should always also contain fringe words.

Pragmatic Organization, on the other hand, focuses on providing maximum vocabulary for a robust system that begins by considering and signaling the intent or function of the message. PODD communication books are the best known of this type of organization. Developed in Australia and originally used in very early intervention and home programs, PODD stands for Pragmatic (the way language is used for social interactions) Organization (the systematic ways words and symbols are arranged) Dynamic Display (pages that change throughout the communication interaction). PODD aims to provide for communicating all of the time, in all environments, on a variety of topics and for a variety of messages. PODD originator Porter stresses the way in which vocabulary and communicating are taught, as well. PODD books contain much of both core and fringe vocabulary.

Topically organized systems arrange words in the system based on topic or category. Categorical and activity- based systems, where vocabulary is organized into pages by category or topic, are still widely in use, but are being more and more transformed into core-based or intent-based systems.

Activity-based systems group words based on the activity or context in which they would be used. A school page, for example, might be created to hold school vocabulary, such as the names of items found there (book, whiteboard, pencil, teacher's names). A zoo page might contain the names of all the animals there and phrases such as "I want to see…" These systems can work when the interaction is very predictable, and the user isn't going to give his own thoughts or ideas.

Unfortunately, that is exactly what we need AAC users to be able to do. Activity or category-based systems might work well as an adjunct to a more robust language-based system; to be used in specific contexts. They also work well as an integrated piece of a dynamic system, as long as the system also contains a method for morphology and syntax development.

According to the American Speech and Hearing Association, (ASHA), the most effective approach to augmenting communication is one that allows for spontaneous, novel utterance generation (SNUG). SNUG allows the AAC user to say whatever he wants, whenever he wants, by constructing messages of words in the same way the rest of us do.

ASHA's website lists the following six points that support the need for SNUG in AAC systems:

In normal language development, young children begin to speak using individual words and word combinations, not full sentences. As language develops, children apply the rules governing the sequencing of language's basic units (i.e. words, word endings, prefixes, etc). to express meaning for a specific communication situation. AAC uses these same basic rules of language.

The vast majority of the sentences we use in our daily communication are sentences that we have never used before in our lifetimes. Furthermore, those sentences have never been spoken by anyone in this history of mankind. That being the case, how could we possibly store in advance the sentences that someone else may wish to speak in the future?

Casual observation of the communication of people who rely on AAC can be made at the many events at which they gather, including conferences and meetings. Pre-stored messages are rarely used in conversations occurring in the natural environment.

Statements by people who rely on AAC clearly indicate that they do not find pre-stored sentences useful for most of what they want to say. Ray Peloquin is typical: "95% of the time, I find myself having to create a sentence, and that's what takes time."

Logged language samples of people who rely on AAC provide the strongest evidence. In various contexts, including clinical and natural conversation settings, logged data suggests that individuals communicating at the highest levels use pre-stored utterances for less than 2% of communication.

In an Australian research project, Sue Balandin and Teresa Iacono (1999) asked speech-language pathologists to predict the topics that would be useful to employees in a sheltered workshop during breaks. The success rate was dismal at less than 10%. If sentences were pre-stored based on these predicted topics, the sentences would have little relevance to the actual conversations occurring.

For toddlers, there are 25 core words that make up more than 95% of what they say. And there are no nouns. Beenajee et al (2003) discovered by observing and recording children in preschools that these 25 words were used most often:

• I	• that	• here
• no	• a	• more
• yes	• go	• out
• my	• mine	• off
• the	• you	• some
• want	• what	• help
• it	• on	• all done
• is	• in	• finished

Combining these initial core words provides access to powerful functions and meanings.

For example, here are only a few of the possibilities:

what that, want that, some that, more that, that mine, it mine, yes mine, off that, that out, want help, it in, it no in, it off, it on, I go, here I go, here it is, on here, want more, is here, is on, is mine, off mine.

If I can teach a student only 1 word initially, I might choose "go," because of the variety of functions it can serve. The student might then be able to say "Go," to go somewhere (i.e. in the wheelchair), to go on the potty, to get in the car and go somewhere, to make it go (turn it on), to start the activity, to ask me to go away and leave him alone, and to say "I go someplace," (all the time).

Focusing on core vocabulary means faster and more functional communication in all environments. The focus on core does not mean, however, that we exclude fringe words altogether. These words can be of the utmost importance to the child. But it does give students automatic access to the most frequently used words; giving him the ability to communicate more easily.

Use of core vocabulary AAC systems allows users to gain better understanding of word meanings, gives them greater diversity of messages in a greater variety of contexts, and allows them to focus on language acquisition rather than access. With the stability of location of vocabulary, and limited need for navigation, users can free up the cognitive energy previously needed to learn discriminations.

Using core words gives users an immediate sense of power - which is what communication is all about. Some of the beginning core words are: stop, go, get, more, turn, mine, on, off, up, down, that. With only these words the AAC user can begin to control what happens to and around him and to control the actions of others. The power of core words is the large number of contexts in which users can use a small number of words.

Simple two-word combinations, using only these words, provides for a significant amount of communication. For example: "get that," "go up," "stop that," "turn that up," "turn that off," "go more," "that mine," "get that down."

Additionally, with the focus on learning core words comes a focus on higher level language acquisition. Use of core teaches users to use descriptive language. Users tell about things/events/people/places, rather than simply, "What." Their messages become longer.

In fact, ASHA's AAC Glossary contains the following: "Communication is based on the use of the individual words of our language. True communication is spontaneous and novel. Therefore, communication systems cannot be based significantly on pre-stored sentences. Communication requires access to a vocabulary of individual words suitable to our needs that are multiple and subject to change. These words must be selected to form the sentences that we wish to say."

Speech-language pathologists should be comfortable with the thought of teaching expanded vocabulary and syntax. Vocabulary and syntax instruction is at the heart of what many of us do much of the time. AAC users need to be taught more kinds of words and how those words are related.

Speech-language pathologists often tend to think of vocabulary in terms of categories and functions. We also look at semantic relationships in terms of synonyms and antonyms, describing and defining words (which take us back to categories and descriptors). Most of the earliest communication books - and many still - are built around basic categorization: things to eat and drink, things to wear, toys to play with, people to name, places to go, some feelings, usually colors and shapes, sometimes letters and numbers. And there continues to be a place for organizing vocabulary that way for specific topics. But how do these combine into phrases and sentences? How do we get beyond labeling and requesting with this vocabulary set?

A developmental concept to consider is the phenomenon of babbling. All young children do it as they are learning language. And, as words form, they put them together in ways that may appear wrong to us, but are 'right' for them as they have perceived the rules, until they acquire a better understanding of those rules. But when we provide only whole messages or single nouns that cannot be combined - or even nouns and verbs with very limited connectability - we don't allow for any way for AAC users to experiment like that.

Oftentimes AAC users are first taught to recognize and use pictures or symbols for concrete objects. The assumption is that concrete items will be more easily understood by, and therefore used by, the beginning AAC user. However, nouns have relatively little use outside of requesting which is, in itself, a "dead end" communication function.

Once a request for an item has been made there is little - or nothing - else to say. Nouns by themselves convey no meaning except as labels, and rarely tell the communicative intent of the user beyond the possibility of requesting.

Core vocabulary, on the other hand, is re-useable vocabulary, and consists of high-frequency words that are used over and over in multiple contexts and with clear meaning. Core words may take more direct instruction and time to learn, but, once learned, can be used in multiple ways across multiple situations.

Symbols for core vocabulary are more abstract than nouns. Verbs may be understood from a symbol, as well as some adjectives and spatial concepts. But many core words are not transparent to the "listener" without reading the label positioned above them. Using context in teaching these words, then, becomes even more important.

Real, authentic experiences in which the word is used will teach the word and its symbol, regardless of the opacity of the symbol itself.

Use of core words allows for access to multiple meaning words to maximize the "real estate." There are only so many symbols any student can use in a single array or page. Using phrases that only work in a single meaning ties up too may spaces with very little communicating messages. Use of core also limits the need for navigating (moving from one page to the next to access needed vocabulary words). It provides for the ability to have stable location of vocabulary for ease of learning. And core words provide access to words from all parts of speech.

Regardless of whether core words will be built one at a time or a dozen at a time, it is important to start with a display that is larger than the beginning point, that is approximately a size that will be functional for the individual for a while. Often 25-36 location grids are used as a starting point. Sometimes larger grids are used. The grid can then have just the single word, or few words, to begin with, using the 'hidden button' feature of many systems; with more core words revealed as language and communication grow.

What is important about this concept is that the vocabulary be placed in its permanent location from the beginning, so that it remains stable throughout learning.

As new words are added, emphasize that new word more than others in Aided Language Stimulation and elicitation strategies. Provide activities that focus on that word more than others, while still maintaining use of words that have been established. Beyond contextual use, begin to add practice activities that practice locating and using the word in both contextual and de-contextual activities. Modify traditional games so that the words needed to play them are the words you've been building.

For students who can't draw to illustrate the meaning of a word - a key vocabulary building activity - cut out pictures from magazines and old books. Have the individual decide if the picture "goes with" (represents or is associated with) the core word or not. Much like Word Walls are used in literacy instruction, Zangari (2013), suggests creating a Core Word Wall with the core words that have been learned. Keep adding to it. You can make this out of a tri-fold science fair display or manila file folders glued together.

Create core word cards and see how many phrases and sentences the individual can make out of them. This will increase as you continue to add core words. As descriptive words are added, they can be used to elaborate on a concept.

Another factor that makes an AAC system robust is the availability of all the parts of speech so that users can create their own novel messages.

As discussed above, focusing on the intent of the message - the why of the message - focuses the child on what kind of words work for which type of situation or intent. Perhaps the best-known and most widely used pragmatic system is the Pragmatic Organized Dynamic Display communication books developed in Australia by Gayle Porter. This system is built on the position that the purpose or intent of the message is the first thing to signal; so that "Something's Wrong" v. "I Like This" sets up the listener for understanding the message, and teaches the user that this kind of word used for this purpose is found [here.]

No Technology AAC:

There are a few things in this "bucket" of components and pieces. Gestures and facial expressions require no technology and nothing, in fact, external to our bodies. We all use gestures and expressions. We shake and nod our heads. We beckon someone to "come here." We smile or frown. These are all communication gestures that we regularly use.

Before all children begin speaking they learn to use communicative gestures. Some of these gestures continue to be extensions or variations on other actions; for example, pointing is a more refined version of reaching. Some gestures are more formal and some, like signs, only become communicative when a group of people assign a consistent meaning to them.

A variety of body movements can be communicative; such as shrugging our shoulders and turning away. We learn to hold up objects for others to see, wave hello and good-bye, hold out two items to give a choice.

Knowing that unintentional behaviors can acquire communicative value through repeated use in routines reminds us that it is not ever too early to begin intervention with AAC. Intervention can begin with a behavior that works for the specific individual for a specific function, and then proceed to shape it into a more conventional response.

More structured systems of gesture include sign languages. There are a number of different sign languages, used in different countries. Here in the U.S. we see both ASL (American Sign Language) and SEE signs (Signing Exact English). In the 1960's and 70's researchers discovered that individuals with intellectual disabilities and autism were able to learn some signs, when they could not learn to speak. While we taught individual signs and sign approximations to these individuals we did not actually teach them "signed language;" which includes many subtleties of spatial, body, and facial cues these students did not learn.

Additionally, most individuals with developmental disabilities and autism using signs use poorly articulated signs as well as idiosyncratic signs. Lack of comprehension by others in the community is a problem for communicating via sign; often even members of the signing communities do not understand poorly articulated signs these individuals use. (Rotholz, Berkowitz, & Burberry 1989).

Stephen Calculator devised a system of Enhanced Natural Gestures (ENGs). These are natural intentional gestures that may already be in the individual's repertoire, or can be easily taught, and that represent what they mean, so are easily understood by others.

ENGs are motor behaviors that are already used by the individual or can be easily taught and are understood by an observer. For example, a student might be taught to hold a cup to his mouth to indicate a desire for a drink.

No tech AAC is also considered to include object-based systems, as well as paper-based systems that may or may not be created with a computer, using letters, words, and/or picture symbols. Paper-based systems are considered no technology pieces, although some paper-based systems require the "technology' of software and printers to create. Once they are assembled on paper, there is no on-going technology used in order to implement them.

These components range in complexity from a single communication symbol to communication books containing well over 100 pages.

Let's take a look at some of these and discuss why they are - or are not - complete and robust AAC systems, and how to use them.

1. Object boards (with or without symbols or text) Object boards are sometimes used for individuals who relate better to concrete objects, or those who have severe vision impairments, or who are deaf-blind, and who have difficulty understanding the symbolic nature of pictures. This often limits those students' available vocabulary and restricts their access to a variety of communicative intents. More recently Erickson (2016) has developed a set of tangible core word symbols using a 3-D printer. These symbols are reproducible, relatively low cost, and relatively easy to make. Those made by Erickson's team have "rules" for parts of speech, which are produced as shape, color, and edging texture. They are taught using the same concepts as all AAC intervention: model, model, model, repeat in a variety of contexts. Symbols are also accompanied by a gesture the child is able to make.

Indications that have been used to determine when individuals can begin to use tangible objects to communicate include:

> The individual has intentional behavior that can be used as a signal to communicate or indicate a symbol.

> The individual understands his ability to control the behavior of the partner through some pre-symbolic behavior.

> The individual is not already using abstract symbols to communicate.

Tangible symbols are real objects, miniature objects, partial objects, or textures. You can hold them and touch them. An individual with vision impairment, one who is deaf-blind, or severely developmentally delayed or with multiple disabilities could discriminate them by feel or texture.

They represent something else and should be used in conjunction with a 2-dimensional symbol support.

Some researchers believe that this progression is necessary for all non-symbolic communicators. Others, such as Porter, believe that children become symbolic communicators by having us use and teach the meanings of those symbols from the beginning.

Single pictures (or photographs) are good for labeling items in the environment or for making simple requests. Even without technological solutions and equipment there is a lot that can be done in classrooms and homes for students who need AAC (but might not yet have it) using pictures taken from software, websites, magazines, or other educational sources.

Picture symbols can be used to teach categorization and to define and describe. They can be used to learn and sort words/symbols by parts of speech. They can be used to teach phonological awareness skills for literacy learners; such as initial and final sounds, word families and rhyming words. They can be used to create word webs to teach vocabulary skills and help to strengthen the connections needed for finding vocabulary within some AAC systems. You can also teach prepositional concepts and the concept of same and different.

Use single pictures to teach a single core vocabulary word. Use 2 pictures to teach a yes/no response or to teach choice-making.

Single communication boards which can be created in several different styles and means of vocabulary organization.

Topic or activity boards are created for specific activities or situations with specific vocabulary. AAC users may be given sets of displays for specific activities used only in the specific environment. These may include menus for restaurants or locations in a specific environment for an outing (such as the animals available to visit at the zoo).

These may increase the speed of communicating in a specific activity by limiting the extraneous vocabulary; but they may also restrict the possibility of off topic comments or functional communication responses.

Speed of communication is often decreased by the need to flip back and forth between multiple pages to combine words for different messages. Individuals often find it difficult to find the words needed for creating messages.

Activity based boards can be placed in the exact site or location in the environment where the activity occurs, rather than keeping them in a single book. However, taking it out of a larger communication book restricts the user from talking about the activity somewhere else or using other vocabulary (such as a request for break, bathroom, other activity, specific person, stating something is wrong, etc.) Another limitation is the instability of vocabulary. Vocabulary moves depending on the activity, and is not always available, hindering the speed of learning.

Phrase-based books are for students whose language is limited and who need quick access to general messages, or for an AAC user to use in social situations whose exchanges have some predictability. These are limiting and are far too often used as a complete AAC system, when they are not.

Pragmatically Organized Dynamic Display Communication Books

PODD books begin by establishing a variety of communicative intents through use of pragmatic branch starters that signal intent or purpose, and provide students with sufficient vocabulary to meet all needs and topics.

In a typical communication book, the navigation usually involves turning the pages one at a time looking for a specific symbol, or needing to remember which categorical page to turn to. Individuals learning to use AAC can become frustrated if they cannot find a specific symbol quickly, and/or distracted as they focus on and point to symbols of interest that are not part of the intended message.

Some simple yet effective features are incorporated into the PODD to improve the efficiency of page turns. These features support communication autonomy by enabling the person using the PODD to (learn to) independently direct movement between pages, even though a partner may physically turn them, at least initially.

Category Based Books Communication books often contain multiple pages organized by category or topic. These frequently lack words other than nouns on their specific category page and some verbs and adjectives; making message construction difficult beyond requests. These are good for students who need visual cues for word retrieval, for students to use during curricular activities whose vocabulary may not be used often.

Behavior cue books These are used for individuals who have Autism Spectrum Disorder or other developmental or behavioral issue. These books provide visual cues for appropriate behavior and are especially helpful during transitions, waiting times, or high demand activities. These books can also include long term visual schedules, sets of transition cues cards, or behavior contingency maps.

Different types of communication books are used for different purposes and/or different models of augmentative/alternative communication. Historically, books have been organized by taxonomy (categories), schema (activities/events), topic, or anecdote (organized by information, scripted narratives or stories).

Because communication books can be used as a part of the AAC system without being the primary component of the system, many creative ways of utilizing them for specific individuals can be found. For example:

Conversation notebooks can be created for users who need access to specific stories to tell, or who need quick access to often-repeated message in social situations. Notebooks can be created, too, with different pages of possible messages for each part of a conversational interaction; such as the attention getter, the topic maintainer, etc.

Core notebooks can contain flip book additions to a core vocabulary board, giving the user access to a variety of sections of topic specific vocabulary. Tabbed flip-through pages can be added to the top of a board, or as fold-out panels on the sides of a board. Fold-out panels can also be used to make a core vocabulary board or book contain more vocabulary.

Often users who are ambulatory don't want bulky communication books - or even devices - to carry with them. A communication book that is wallet-sized can be very handy. They might be used when the individual is going out to a specific location or event. They are often used by teens and adults with developmental disabilities who don't want anything obtrusive and need to provide basic identification information, as to meet basic needs in the community. Wallet-sized books are also handy for people who are primarily verbal, but are not well-understood by unfamiliar listeners. They can fit in a pocket or handbag and used as needed.

Students who are active and spend time on the playground or playing out of doors don't want to carry a big communication book or device with them while they are climbing the monkey bars, playing handball, or going down a slide - nor would a device be safe in many playground situations. Creating a small number of picture strips or picture mini-pages that are placed on a ring and hung from the individual's belt loop are useful in these situations.

Low Technology

Low tech options include a variety of simple switches and battery-operated devices. These typically have 1, 2, or up to 32 buttons - or cells - for storing words or messages. The largest number of cells in a low-technology device is 128 on the AMDi 128, but devices with fewer cells are seen more often.

These are called static display devices because the display does not change until someone physically removes and replaces the picture overlay. Some static display devices have multiple levels so that, when the level is changes, the overlay can be changed without having to re-record messages. Six or eight different picture display overlays can be created and stored with the device, so that simply by moving a switch to change the level for the recorded speech the user can change the communication display for a different topic.

Examples of static display devices include:

* BIGmack/LITTLEmack - A single button with a single recorded message. You can provide the user with a single message the can be used for gaining attention (in a noisy environment or when the person is in a different room), asking for help (in getting to the bathroom, in getting dressed, etc.), protesting, making a single request that fit the environment (i.e. by the door to ask to go out).

   A single message can make a request, greet others, accept or reject, to protest, to direct, to start or end an activity, to indicate possession, and to participate. You can also program the button with a line from a repetitive text, with the direction to 'turn the page,' or with the punchline from a joke.

   You can also use it to teach a single core word; such as "help," "more," "stop," "go," "play," "eat," "drink," and others.

* iTwo 2 message buttons can be used to answer yes/no, ask for more/stop, make a choice between 2 items or activities, get attention/ask to be alone.

* Talking photo albums can be used for shopping lists, picture recipes, telling a personal narrative (about an event or experience), give personal information, direct the steps of an activity, present a book report or other presentations in class, take attendance, sing a song or otherwise participate in class.

These may be used for gaining attention, making a request, giving a greeting, or participating in reading a repeated line book. (see Resources for Adaptivation's list of 100 ways to use a BigMack or Sequencer)

Another simple AAC solution is the Talking Photo Album, originally marketed by Radio Shack for the general public.

Ways to use a Talking Photo Album are also found on Adaptivation' s site: (note: not limited to photos; also use PCS, ticket stubs and activity receipts, etc.)

* shopping list (can use product labels or photos)

* picture recipes

- retelling an event

- presenting personal information

- telling the steps to a task or activity

- flash cards

- picture menu

- speech or book report

- attendance

- singing a song

- sharing a collection with friends

- creating social stories

- picture identification

- current events

- simple dictionary

- reminder list for chores

- play scripts

Sequencer and Randomizer buttons - The sequencer sequences messages in order, for the user to engage in a greetings exchange, tell a joke, give directions, tell a story, "read" a short book, or give a presentation. They can be used to provide the sequence of steps to an activity or recipe, to tell a story, to sing along. They can be used in multiple ways at "Calendar time

The randomizer holds multiple versions of the same messages, so that it appears fresh each time; i.e. Hi, Hello, Hey there, Yo. When used for that type of greeting, it prevents the user from sounding stiff and repetitive. Buttons that provide multiple messages in random order can also be used to take attendance, to greet others with a variety of different greetings (hi, hello, yo, what's up, hey there, etc.) They can also be used in games such as Simon Says and BINGO.

Adaptivation, Inc. has the following lists of suggestions on their website for use of the Sequencer button: recite poems, tell a joke, recite days or months, trick or treat, announce today's lunch menu, talk to Santa, read a story, complain, introduce someone, buy a movie ticket, count, rent a video, recite the Pledge of Allegiance, shop for clothes, give a shopping list to a clerk, play a game, present spelling test words, add sound effects to a story, order in a restaurant, direct a game, take attendance, tell how-to give the weather report, play Duck- Duck- Goose, direct P.E. activity, tell about a field trip, sing songs, give recipe instructions, tell about a vacation, play Simon Says, give a book report, play 20 Questions, Show & Tell, pack a lunch, directions, conduct an interview, give clues in a guessing game, deliver a message, match sounds to pictures, give announcements, give a phone number, request assistance, direct self-care activities, call for a taxi, call to order a pizza, repositioning directions, cleaning room, steps for a project, directions from place to place, recite alphabet, call a pet to dinner.

* Hip Talker, Wrist Talker, Go Talk - These are only a few of the simple static devices that can be used for basic, functional communication responses. Responses for gaining attention, indicating the need for assistance or the bathroom or a break or a change in activity are helpful to put on these simple devices. The Go Talk devices are available in 9, 12, 20, and 32 message configurations. The larger arrays can be used for more functional activity boards.

In general, static display devices can be useful for choice making and for making responses in specific situations or activities, i.e. classroom calendar time, read-aloud reading time, playing with a toy, arts & crafts.

Simple ideas for static device use in the inclusive classroom:

Simple static display devices can be used in many classrooms for specific curricular activities:

- Teachers can ask a binary choice or multiple-choice questions, which the student can answer with a yes/no response or by locating a), b), c), or d).

- Students can move items around, providing the physical movements, while the AAC user needs only to say, "Put it there."

- Program story elements onto a device and have the AAC user respond with the appropriate element.

- Or program events in history, and have the AAC user participate in putting them in temporal order.

Simple ideas for static device use in the home:

- Place a single message button by the front or back door so child can ask to go outside or for a walk.

- Place a single or dual message button on the table at mealtimes; the child can ask for more or for something different, and specify whether to eat or to drink.

- In the bedroom, use a static display device with articles of clothing and colors, to make dressing time faster.

- In the bathroom, have a laminated board on the bathroom wall; use it to provide Aided Input for the sequence of body parts to wash. Also have "hot" and "cold" symbols so children can tell about the temperature and/or have it changed.

- In the bathroom, have picture sequences for all tasks needed.

- In the kitchen, have displays for specific snacks or foods the child likes. Make sure to include comments; such as "I like it," "I don't like it," "more," "all done," and "I want different."

- In the T.V. room (whichever room that might be), have choices of favorite shows, movies, and DVDs. Again, make sure to include comments, such as, "I want different," "watch again," "watch with me," "that's funny," etc.

- At play time, have choices of toys available

However, static displays:

- lack sufficient vocabulary to meet many communication needs,

- often only have enough vocabulary for the specific activity,

- often have no room for off-topic messages, clarifications,

- usually have no flexibility for genuine message construction,

- may frequently change the location of vocabulary from overlay to overlay; obviating learning through automaticity, motor planning,

- and most require access through direct selection; only a few can be used with switch scanning access for students with physical impairments

That's not to say that static display devices don't have a place in the classroom or therapy situations - or at home if possible. Just that they rarely make sense as a primary or only piece of the AAC system.

What can you do with just 1 symbol?

- ✓ request (I want) - want, that, give, get
- ✓ greet (Hi) - hi, hello, hey there, bye
- ✓ accept or reject (don't want) - yes, no, don't, not
- ✓ protest (stop) - stop, not, don't, away
- ✓ direct (there) - here, give, get, put

- ✓ cessation or continuation (stop, more) - different, go

- ✓ possession (mine) - my, mine, your, his

- ✓ participation (not my cat) - yes, no, repeating line, specific response.

Print out pages of category related nouns, verbs, words that associate or locate together. Laminate them and cut them apart. Now you have a picture library of cards you can put in specific locations, use for learning games, have students sort or assemble messages for practice.

At home you can use these symbols to label what's in drawers or cabinets or the fridge.

At school, use them to teach counting, defining, describing, using prepositions, creating phrases and sentences, identifying first/last sound, identifying synonyms and antonyms, grouping them by category, making word webs, making story maps, sorting by category or attribute, identifying as same or different, creating fill in the blank activities, and using with scenes to match, name, place while following directions, understanding prepositional concepts, identifying what doesn't belong. These activities can apply to any age or grade level or classroom type.

What can I do with just 1 message button?

- ✓ Program it with the repeated line from a book, add a representational symbol on top, cue the student to activate the device to help read the story.

- ✓ Record "turn the page," or "let me."

- ✓ Record a greeting, a joke, a direction, a lunch choice, an attention-getting phrase.

- ✓ Say, "I need a break."

- ✓ Teach a single core word: help, more, stop, go, all done, don't, make, play, eat, drink, read, sleep.

Tell me again what can I do with a talking photo album?

- ✓ make a shopping list
- ✓ make picture recipes
- ✓ retell a personal narrative/experience
- ✓ direct the steps of an activity
- ✓ make a picture menu
- ✓ take attendance
- ✓ sing a song
- ✓ create a social story,
- ✓ make a simple dictionary

There are two widely used organizational systems for arranging vocabulary on these static displays (Elder and Goosens):

1. Order of activity - This is usually used with displays of 9 buttons or less. Vocabulary words/messages are organized in the order they're needed for the specific activity; the sequence of events or steps in the activity. Vocabulary/messages are chosen based on what's most highly prioritized in an exchange during that specific activity or topic. The focus is on cause/effect and sequencing objectives.

2. Fitzgerald key format - uses syntactic order of vocabulary. Words that appear on multiple boards should always be in the same location, opposite concepts should be placed next to each other (horizontally or vertically), nouns should be organized by category/subcategory.

High-tech

High-tech refers to more complex, computer-based devices. Dedicated Devices are manufactured specifically for AAC use and nothing else. These devices use touch screen technology to allow for finger point access, and are referred to as dynamic display devices because large numbers of pages can be linked together for fast and easy transition from one page of vocabulary/messages to another.

Dynamic display devices are typically based on a standard computer or tablet, which has been specifically modified by the manufacturer with software, protective casing, and other specific capabilities.

Dynamic display devices range in size from hand held palm sized (5" screens) to lightweight portable devices with handles and mid-sized screens (usually 7-8" but also 10" screens), and full-sized screens (typically 12" - 15") that are usually used on table tops or mounted on wheelchairs or rolling stands.

Most high-tech devices can be accessed by direct touch or a switch. Many also can be activated by head mouse or eye gaze technology. The computer allows the device to be programmed to scan through items on a page in a variety of patterns and at adjustable speeds, with selections made through one or two switches, or using a joystick, or other adapted input method. Addition of a specific module for reading eye movement can also allow input via eye gaze.

High-tech devices can have only 1 or 2 buttons per page or more than 100. These devices contain software that comes pre-loaded on them that provides various pre-determined page sets for children at various levels of development as well as for adults with various needs. Part of the purpose of an assessment that recommends a high-tech device is to determine the specific page set that a user or potential user should be using. AAC users with adequate language skills can participate in this decision.

The range of available high-tech devices has narrowed recently, with the increased use of iOS devices and AAC apps for communication. The remaining systems and their software make some assumptions about AAC users that need to be remembered when considering an AAC device for a given individual.

While the range of high-tech devices themselves all have similar features and capabilities, the software that organizes the vocabulary and presents it in page sets can be significantly different from one device to the next. Often, within a single device, the software contains multiple different page sets designed to meet the needs of different users at different levels of linguistic and communicative competence.

While this provides a range of choice meant to meet users' varying needs, it too often happens that a limiting page set is chosen for users with limited skills and progress is restricted to the capabilities of that particular vocabulary set. In other words, too often competence is not assumed and therefore not developed.

At the most complex level, a keyboard on a computer or tablet, or a text-to-speech only device assumes the greatest level of language and literacy. The user needs to understand language at the phonological level, where he constructs messages by constructing words, then phrases, and sentences. [Not all users of text-to-speech actually understand sufficient language to generate sentences in this way; for example: autistics with hyperlexic skills may be able to read and write/type words, but generally do so without understanding what they are reading or how to join the words into comprehensible structures. There are intervention strategies that can stimulate and expand the generation of linguistic functions and syntactic forms.

Among high-tech systems are differing ways of structuring access to symbols in order to facilitate message generation. Most systems that are widely used are word-based systems, with a variety of organizational patterns. The list of available systems is changing rapidly as companies rally to save the market for speech generating devices, in the face of competition from iOS devices and AAC apps.

iOS Devices Used as AAC Devices

The relatively low cost and ease of access to iOS devices, including iPhones, iPad Minis and iPads, has led to their use ever-increasingly as AAC devices.

Putting an AAC app onto a commercially available device bypasses the lengthy evaluation and funding process. However, without a good, comprehensive AAC evaluation, it is easy to choose a system that is not ultimately the best for a given student. Knowing that AAC evaluators can be hard to come by, I still implore you to have a comprehensive evaluation.

One particular advantage to the use of iOS devices as AAC devices is their appeal. Light, et al (2005) have noted that many dedicated AAC devices have been designed more from the adult than a child's perspective and lack visual appeal. But devices that are more interesting and age appropriate may be used more and abandoned less. Oftentimes, when it is not possible to get an adolescent to use an AAC system that makes him look too different from his peers, use of a ubiquitous iOS device is accepted both by the user and his peers.

Unfortunately, it is often forgotten in a rush to adopt the newest technology or lower the cost that one size does not fit all, and determination of an appropriate AAC system must come after an appropriate assessment.

It must be remembered that selecting an AAC app is a part of the assessment process as a whole, that is a dynamic, structured process of defining the user's strengths, abilities, needs are matched to the features of various AAC systems. As Shane and Costello warn, the iDevice must be matched and fitted to the user; not the user "fitted" to the device (Gosnell, Costello, Shane).

There are some specific issues that accompany the use of this technology for AAC:

1. Unfortunately, there is often no one to guide the purchaser in selecting an appropriate AAC app for the end user, and no one to support the user once the device is purchased.

   Communication partners do not always know how to program or customize the app appropriately for the user. Whereas dedicated communication device manufacturers provide individualized training and support, as well as technical support, these are not usually available with tablet devices.

Ultimately, without appropriate training and intervention the device is not any more useful than a more expensive dedicated device would have been, and the problem is not solved.

We cannot just put a device in front of the user and expect them to begin to communicate. The AAC system - whether it is low tech or high-tech - is only a tool. The user needs to learn how to use the tool. Without instruction the tool is often worthless, and - even worse - leads to abandonment of AAC.

2. Physical access is a significant issue with iOS technology. It must be determined not only whether the individual can use an isolated finger to point to/activate the buttons of the device, but also whether he can swipe and pinch.

Key guards, while available for iOS devices and AAC apps are difficult to connect to the devices and keep in place. Because the device itself is not designed to hold a key guard they are often too easily disturbed and dislocated by users with spasticity or other motor issues; making them useless.

Switch scanning is more recently available for the iPad as AAC device. Specific AAC apps have specific capabilities for using scanning with Bluetooth switch access.

3. The multi-functionality of iOS devices are also an issue.

As opposed to dedicated devices that serve only one purpose - communication - iOS users have come to expect access to all of the other things that can be done on an iPad.

For users who are easily distracted, access to games, videos, and more leads them out of the AAC system and away from communicating. It is not possible to continue to communicate, when needed, while playing a game or music or watching a video.

Users with ASD in particular are often so focused on watching videos or specific apps on the iPad that they frequently exit out of the AAC app.

While the devices have a feature that allows the partner to lock the device into a specific app, this can cause behavior problems in some individuals who have come to expect access to those other features.

4. It can be overwhelming to try to differentiate between AAC apps and choose the "right" one for the user.

At last count there were well over 200 AAC apps available in the iTunes store. However, the vast majority of these apps are little more than electronic choice boards. Most are not nearly robust enough to offer sufficient vocabulary to meet all of a user's communication needs.

Among the decisions that need to be made to match the user and an AAC app, the following features of apps need to be considered:

- Whether the app has voice output that is synthesized or digitized and ability to adjust the voice output, that is, adjust rate pitch, type of synthesized voice used (male, female, appropriate accent)

- Ability to speak after each word or sentence or only when the entire message is selected from the message window

- What symbol set(s) are provided

- Ability to import additional graphics and ability to adjust the display for button size, array size, background color, button color, button border color, font size, and color

- The availability to access multiple modes, e.g. grid display, visual scene, key board

- Availability of key board with word prediction

- Ability to use abbreviation expansion, "recents" list, and/or grammatical prediction or selection

- Ability to access via scanning, to use zoom feature with direct selection, to adjust dwell time for direct selectors, and/or ability to use select on release rather than select on touch

A variety of app matrixes exist, showing the apps and their features. Children's Hospital of Boston, Call Scotland, Spectronics in Oz, and the PrAACtical AAC blog are 4 four of the most comprehensive.

Color Coding AAC Systems

Whether the AAC system uses paper-based or technology-based pages, there are two or three main alternate color-coding systems used in AAC systems to code parts of speech; the Fitzgerald and Modified Fitzgerald Keys and the Goosens, Crain, and Elder System. The button, the button border, or the text of the button can be color coded.

It doesn't matter which system you choose to use in a communication book or display, as long as there is consistency among parts of the AAC system. Do not use a different set of color codes in the communication book than is used on the user's device. Color coding provides an additional visual cue to aid with vocabulary organizing and locating.

Studies (Thistle and Wilkinson 2009) determined that clustering of symbols by like-color aided in the speed and efficiency of locating symbols on a display. Foreground color in particular had a positive influence, while background color alone had a negative impact on location of symbols.

Color coding of the buttons allows the user and facilitator to locate symbols more easily. If color-coding is organized according to grammatical categories, the user has an added feature to assist in learning how to sequence symbols, and to support the development of sentence-building (syntax). According to the most recent best practice, because shape is a salient clue we should color-code the background, not the figure, so that the shape of the symbol will be more visible to the student.

A display should be organized as follows from the left side of the overlay to the right side:

Musslewhite suggests using the Goosens, Crain and Elder color-coding system:

Verbs - words which tell action {i.e. Open, Come, Eat} PINK

Descriptors - adjectives and adverbs {i.e. Pretty, Slow, Red} BLUE

Prepositions - position words {i.e. In, Off} GREEN

Nouns - person, place or thing {Cat, Hat, John} YELLOW

Miscellaneous - Wh-words questions Who, What, How, Exclamations interjections, etc. {i.e. Uh Oh, Wow}, Negative Words negations {i.e. No, Don't}, Pronouns; personal, possessive {I, You} ORANGE

While many systems use the Goosens, et al, system, many others continue to use the modified Fitzgerald coloring system, described below. Historically, most big tech devices have used the **Fitzgerald system:**

People/pronouns – he, she YELLOW

Verbs/action words – go, want GREEN

Adjectives - big, little DARK BLUE

Adverbs - slow, fast LIGHT BLUE

Prepositions - in, out PURPLE

Determiners - this, that ORANGE

Interjections – please, thank you PINK

Nouns - pretzel, mom ORANGE

Wh words - who, what, where RED

Conjunctions - and, but, or WHITE

Modified Fitzgerald Key:

Blue: Adjectives

Green: Verbs

Yellow: Pronouns

Orange: Nouns

White: Conjunctions

Pink: Prepositions, social words

Purple: Questions

Brown: Adverbs

Red: Important function words, negation, emergency words

Grey: Determiners**

What do you need to know about color coding? Probably not a lot. If your student/child has a robust system, it will already be color coded with whichever system the manufacturer/developer has used. Simply continue to follow this as you add buttons. If you are starting out with a paper-based system, it also may already come with a color-coding system; such as the PODD books do.

So, now that you have the basics about AAC components, let's talk about how you decide on a system for an individual, and how to implement communication strategies.

CHAPTER 4

AAC Assessment Strategies

"The ultimate goal or outcome is to design a system that matches a child's abilities and communication needs. Components of the system should enable the child not only to communicate, but also develop expressive language performance."

— Bruno (2005)

The assessment process itself is not a difficult one, when clinicians are prepared to keep specific features of each system in mind while interacting with the student. As a professional, you are the "expert" when it comes to language development and strategies to teach more language. As a parent, you are the "expert" on your child. As a team, you need to come together to determine where the child is now, where you want him to be, and how to get there; with a united front and consistent implementation.

Parents: assist with the process by providing the clinician with information about how the child is currently communicating. Tell the clinician how your child makes requests for objects, for activities, for assistance, for getting out of a task or situation, how he greets others, gives an opinion, answers yes/no, protests. Does your child use facial expressions, proxemics (standing or sitting near the desired target), gestures or signs? As a parent, you know more about how he communicates, what he prefers, and what engages him.

By the end of the session(s) some of the questions that need to be answered include:

- Can the individual answer yes/no and/or Wh-questions consistently?

- Can he recognize and understand symbols to be used in an AAC system?

- Can he use single message buttons, a sequence of symbol buttons, a combination of symbol buttons and/or typing or text-to-speech generation alone?

- Can the individual find a symbol button only on the visible page, or can he navigate between pages to find the word or message needed?

- Can he combine symbols to generate language?

- Does he initiate or only respond?

- Does he use only noun referents (object names) or can he use more general/core vocabulary?

- What are his language abilities in the areas of form, content, and use?

- Which communication intents does he use, which are emerging, which are stimulable?

- Does the individual have the physical capacity to use an AAC system to achieve functional communication, or are access options needed?

- Which alternate modes of access can he use or learn to use?

- If the individual has a visual impairment, can he process visual input, discriminate symbols, and/or need considerations for contrast, light, movement?

- How does he communicate during familiar and/or motivating activities?

- How does he communicate with different partners?

Ultimately, what we are looking for is to:

- define the child's skills and abilities in language (both current skills and extending possibilities)

- physical abilities in hearing, vision, and physical access modality

- responses to environmental demands

- partners' skills

- symbol type and size

- array size

- grammatical skills and potential

- navigation skills through categorization

- syntax sequencing skills and potential

- ability to access available vocabulary

- use of morphology, if available

- use of different communication functions

Note that the absence of any of these skills is NOT a reason why the child cannot use AAC/symbolic communication. This simply tells us where the student is currently so that we can plan our intervention. There is no cognitive level that defines the child's ability to use AAC at all, or a specific type of AAC.

ASHA's policy on cognitive referencing - otherwise known as the discrepancy model - is strong, as I said earlier.

This becomes a bigger issue for nonspeaking students than for those with speech; as we are unlikely to know exactly what a child can do given correct instruction if we ban them from the "game" before they even start.

Students with significant disabilities are often denied access to services and supports because their language and cognitive skills are believed to be commensurate. But this gives the impression that communication skills only warrant intervention when language skills are "below" a student's cognitive skills. (Miller & Chapman, 1980; Shane & Bashir, 1980).

Newborns communicate. Communication, in and of itself, does not require linguistic skills. And what children can do with structured intervention often far exceeds our expectations; telling us loudly and clearly that we are not expecting enough. That we need to presume competence.

ASHA's position statement concludes:

"Evidence from research has shown that all individuals can benefit from appropriate communication services to improve the effectiveness of their communication. A child's cognitive age relates to where along the continuum of communication he or she will begin the communication and language process. A child's cognitive age should not be used to deny communication services and supports.

People used to believe that individuals had to demonstrate certain cognitive skills before they would be able to benefit from communication services. Recent research has shown that communication and language develop from early infancy along with cognitive and thinking skills. In fact, sometimes teaching new communication skills can help a child develop other thinking skills.

The position of the National Joint Committee for the Communication Needs of Persons with Severe Disabilities is an official policy of the **American Speech-Language-Hearing Association.**

It states that determining eligibility on pre-formulated criteria, rather than the specific individual's needs, environment, response to intervention, and supports may violate federal statute and state laws.

There is a reason why this is often referred to as the "wait to fail" model of intervention. But just why do we need to wait for the student to fail before providing intervention that could have prevented such failure?

Nickola Wolf Nelson suggests we ask, not who can benefit from intervention based on their IQ, but, "Who has language and communication skills that are insufficient to support them in the important contexts of their lives?" She cites the evidence from Lahey (1992), Cole (1990, 1992), & Terrell (1978) that:

1. Cognitive and language tests may reflect the same things;

2. Some combinations of language tests and cognitive tests show a discrepancy when others may not—and at some times, but not others;

3. Formal testing often yields biased results for children from diverse cultural and linguistic communities;

4. Formal tests fail to assess contextually-based needs for language intervention;

5. Validity for determining the need for language intervention services is questionable; and,

6. Children can benefit from language intervention services whether or not they show discrepancies

Students should be served based on their unmet communication needs. Communication is a basic need and a basic right, says the National Joint Committee for Communication Needs of Persons with Severe Disabilities (1992).

Gayle Porter speaks about the "Catch 22" of AAC assessments, and it's imperative you keep this in mind as you assess.

"We can only see what the individual is doing with what is provided. If we think this is all they can do, we don't provide anything more. If we don't provide anything more, the individual never learns more."

It is crucial that the focus on assessments (and intervention) stay on the communication aspect; not on speech itself. This means a focus on shared meaning between communication partners. It also means avoiding "testing" instead of engaging with and communicating with the child. We no longer say, "Touch the dog," "Touch the one you read," "Touch pants" after navigating to clothing.

We should also remember, while evaluating, that AAC is a system of multiple components. The AAC system can include gestures and signs, pictures/symbols/letters, facial expressions and body language, eye gaze, speech generating devices, and partners who facilitate genuine communication.

The assessment should consider communication contexts and partners as well as current skills. The difference between the two will guide you in determining what this child wants or needs to communicate that they currently cannot (this is where parents are particularly important to the process), who does or might this child want to communicate with that they cannot, what type of communication situations does this child need to communicate in that they cannot now?

Make an inventory of the student's current use of:

- speech, word approximation, vocalizations

- any current AAC system (including devices, books, boards, symbol use

- gestures, proxemics (placing one's self near the item/activity desired) body language

- facial expressions

- eye gaze

Observations of the student are important. Both parents and professionals should take an objective look at their respective environments. Is all learning and doing teacher or parent directed? Is there ample opportunity in the environment for the child to communicate? Does the teacher, SLP, or parent offer choices? Does the communication partner wait for a response? (We tend to jump in too soon with a response if we think the child cannot do it; rather than waiting for processing and formulating time). Does the teacher/SLP/parent ask open-ended questions? Sometimes, the lack of student response is a function of the communication partner's behavior rather than the child's abilities.

You should also look at what vocabulary the student has access to. Is it sufficient for successful participation in the classroom, home, or community activity? Is it available permanently or only taken out at specific times? Is the student engaged? Physical presence is not the same as active participation.

While there are no standardized evaluation protocols for AAC evaluation, there are a couple of tools worth using. One is The Communication Matrix, by Charity Rowland. It consists of an extensive series of questions that pinpoints exactly where and how a child is communicating, and provides a structural framework for moving forward. The form is also available from: http://www.designtolearn.com.

The on-line tool moves you through each stage and skill, page by page, and then generates a clear visual profile of the individual's current communication skills. Because of the visual nature of the framework, understanding where to set goals is clear.

The matrix is designed for individuals whose skills are at the 0-24-month level, and accommodates any and all forms of communication, regardless of the complexity of the communication disorder. It addresses the 4 basic reasons to communicate: to obtain what we want, refuse what we don't want, engage in social interaction, and provide or request information. Within each of those areas is a series of questions about why and how the individual communicates. The matrix addresses communication behaviors from pre-intentional, intentional, unconventional and conventional communication, through symbolic communication and early language development. https://www.communicationmatrix.org.

The Augmentative and Alternative Communication Profile, published by LinguiSystems and designed by Tracy Kovach, provides a checklist for evaluation of operational, linguistic, social, and strategic areas of AAC use and learning; the four area of competence listed by Janice Light. It provides for test-retest data on the same form and uses a numerical rating system for a variety of sub skills in those four major areas of AAC competence.

One thing we do not want to do in AAC implementation is to make the child move from no tech to low tech to high-tech solutions. Providing speech output gives a clear intent to the communication partners. High-tech systems usually (with the exception of PODD) provide better opportunities for scaffolding and modeling; only Partner Assisted Scanning provides more feedback and models. Voice output provides auditory feedback while learning symbol meaning; unlike no tech solutions. And, most importantly, making the child learn multiple systems this way only makes learning to communicate **more** difficult.

There has been a paradigm shift; moving away from evaluating only picture discrimination, array size, and other skills out of any context. This provides a "testing" situation, rather than a "communicating" one, and we often miss just how much the child communicates.

AAC assessment has instead shifted to a "participation model" (Beukelman & Mirenda 2005). Identify contexts that are interactive, motivating, meaningful, and high frequency. Use genuine activities to engage the student, providing sufficient vocabulary with which to interact. Assess participation patterns and communication needs during typical interaction in natural settings.

This model is based on functional participation requirements of typical peers. It is designed to assess and intervene across all environments and provides opportunities for multiple communication functions. Choose materials and activities that motivate the child. Provide sufficient symbols representing people, actions, locations, comments, and social interactions of that activity. Don't just use the immediate targets the child is working to learn; model the next level and above for adult models of expansion (Kaiser, 2012). By using genuine activities to engage the individual while providing sufficient vocabulary with which to interact, we can get a better picture of what he can do currently and what he has the potential to do with scaffolding.

This model is consistent with the ecological approach, which looks at the individual's functioning in relationship to the environment and its activities within which he must function or participate. It was originally developed by Brown, et al (1979) and Brown (1984) who proposed looking at the individual in every environment and activity in which the he is involved and examining how the individual participates (if at all) and how that participation could be developed and increased. The focus is on how the individual can be independent, included, and satisfied within his daily activities and environments.

The ecological approach lends itself to communication skills easily, in looking at how the individual is able to participate in his environments in terms of ability to gain control over his environment, regulate social engagement and interactions, and give and receive information. The focus is on assessing and then developing communication skills in the context of natural daily environments. Current activities, as well as those in which the individual is expected to participate in the near future, are the focus.

Genuine assessment means meaningful activities, motivating activities, and genuine communication contexts. Start with something the child likes to do; such as blowing bubbles, watching a video, talking about sports, make something (picture, block castle, birdhouse), read a favorite book, do a make-over/manicure, engage in the student's area of obsession.

In the process of the activity we do need to look for whether or not the student can discriminate pictures (photos, icons, high contrast colors) in arrays of 2…4…8…20…84.

Can he use a single icon or sequence 2, 3, 5 icons in a grammatical phrase or sequence multiple single symbols to provide a complete but telegraphic message? (Telegraphic messages are those that contain key words, but omit things like a, the, and, and other articles, conjunctions and similar "small" words).

Provide a variety of activity options. Often, I have students who choose "watch." I then provide a choice of movie options. I put the disc in the DVD player (best investment ever for clinicians). Then I wait with an expectant look on my face; a nonverbal cue for "What should I do?" As needed, I'll give the least prompt needed to get to "go" or "turn on." We watch for a brief bit, then I pause it. Again, I give the expectant face and, if needed, use the least prompt to get "more," or "movie." Depending on the child, I might start by putting the wrong movie in the player and model "different." While watching, I model comments, such as "I like it," or "funny."

I use a lot of bubbles. They seem to be an almost universal motivator. I find the best bubbles are the ones from Gymboree. (I have no financial relationship with them, I simply love their bubbles. They have no soap to get in eyes, and stay intact a lot longer than traditional bubbles).

Model "blow" or "go." Model "more." Model "you do" vs "I do." Model "big bubble," "pop bubbles," "blow bubbles," and "all done." When finished with bubbles, the child can navigate to different activities. If they can navigate back to the activities page can they navigate to other pages?

Nail polish is big with teen girls. Words and phrases to model include; "that one" (color), "different" (color), "oops," "mess," "fix it," "put it on," "take off," "I like," "I don't like," "like yours," "pretty," "do more."

Any interactive play situation can generate similar vocabulary. Even activities that are usually solitary - like puzzles - can become interactive if sabotage is used (help, more pieces, different). Sabotage; deliberately obstructing access (to something), is a great strategy in both assessment and implementation. It should not be used all the time or in every activity; we don't want frustration. But used judiciously, putting items just out of reach or giving too little or giving the wrong thing, can produce more communication in students.

Playing, eating, watching are oftentimes the best situations for assessment. But if none of these is motivating for your child, try, "I need break," or "leave me alone." Model use and then honor the request repeatedly. I once followed a young man all around his house with a device (which I knew he had some experience using) and told him as he walked away from me repeatedly, "tell me to leave." When he finally did so, I left.

You might also try various sensory stimuli and model 'go' 'stop' 'more' 'different' 'again' 'want do' 'want that' 'do that' 'do again' and 'get,'

No matter how unmotivated your student appears to be by anything, he has some communicative behaviors. Find them. Use them. Replace them.

I recently evaluated a young man (age 14) who has severe quadriplegic cerebral palsy, and who had no communication system. School staff thought there was nothing they could do. In fact, even the mom was a bit skeptical at the evaluation, saying, "He won't pay attention to that. He doesn't like technology or things. He just likes people."

I could work with that. The manufacturer's representative who had brought an eye gaze system for him to try programed a simple "Simon Says" activity. The grin on his face when he discovered he could make us sit down, stand up, turn around, and dance was amazing!

Assessment and implementation with AAC is all about pushing the "Zone of Proximal Development" (Vygotsky 1934).

If he used 1 word/symbol, can I get him to use 2? If he used the page displayed, can I get him to navigate to another page once - or twice? If he's using only 1 core word, can I add another?

Determining an appropriate system that matches the features of any given system with the strengths and needs of the user needs to consider all variables. The system must be matched to the user's needs motorically, linguistically, visually and motivationally, and to the supports available in the environment. Promote a sense of control as much as possible in the AAC user by including him in the process whenever possible. This may include the individual's ability to prefer (and articulate his preference of) one system over another, or simply to match the color of the device housing to the color of the user's wheelchair. Including vocabulary that is important to the user also needs to be a part of the matching process.

One of the important factors to look for, too, is the variety of communication functions the child uses. This can include requesting (of objects, activity, attention, assistance, recurrence, and information), asking, answering, directing actions of others, commenting, protesting, greeting.

For each of these functions, we want to look for the mode the child is currently using; intentional and unintentional gestures/actions/expressions, other gestures, symbolic vs non- symbolic, concrete vs abstract symbols, and symbols combined to language structures.

There are many communication functions; however, often the AAC user gets stuck at a requesting stage and is not helped to progress. Particularly consider what communication the individual uses beyond requesting:

greet	hi, hello, what's up, yo, hey
part	bye, see you later, good-bye
affirm	yes, ok, I agree, that's right
reject	stop, all done, no more, finished, no, not
negation	no, not, stop, not that
cessation	stop, no more
request assistance	help, I need help, I need you
request recurrence	again, more, do again
request information	what, why, when, where, who
request object	that, this, the, it
request action	want, get, give, do, turn, put, open, close

direct	go, get, help, come, up, try, there
redirect	different, another
existence	that, there, look, it
nonexistence	none, not
disappearance	all gone, away
possession	mine, your, his, hers
commenting	like, don't like, bad, good, silly, mean
describing	fat, tall, cold, hot, fast, under, between
person	I, you, him, mom, dad, grandma
interjection	Cool!, No way!, Wow! How about that? Darn!
Questioning	Who?, What?, Where?, When?, Why?, How much?, How?

Throughout the assessment clinicians need to look at the difference between skills and needs:

What does or might the individual need to communicate that he cannot?

Who does he want to communicate with that he cannot?

What type of situations might he need to communicate in that he cannot?

What vocabulary does the individual currently have available to him?

What vocabulary do the various systems being considered have to offer?

Is it sufficient for successful participation?

Is it sufficient to meet all needs; including functional off-topic and social comments?

Is it available permanently?

Does it allow for genuine communication in the environment; especially school and work environments?

How should that vocabulary be organized? Will a core word system that limits navigation and focuses on use of a smaller number of reusable words work for him, or can he use a system with a larger vocabulary of core and fringe words, but will rely upon a partner to assist him with autonomous communication? How will the organization of vocabulary impact his autonomy? Will he be independent?

ASSESSMENT SNAPSHOT

R.J. was a 5-year-old boy with autism.

He was very interested in Thomas the Train and loved watching Thomas movies. There wasn't much else that engaged him.

This was a boy who had only experience with a limited array of symbols Velcro'd to a board from which he could choose reinforcers during break times in class, and at snack time.

He had difficulty navigating from a "home" page by choosing "want" or "watch" to get to a choice of activities. From the choice of activities, he was able to choose the "DVD." He was then on the page of DVD choices where he easily found "Thomas." I went back to the home page and modeled "go," then turned it on.

Once the movie was on, I tried lowering the volume, and modeling "Turn it up," but R.J. wasn't as interested in listening to it as he was in seeing it. After a minute he just reached over to the DVD player and turned it up himself. We watched for several minutes, then I hit the pause button. I began by modeling "Thomas." When he followed the model, I turned it back on. The next time, I backed out of the DVD choices page and went back to the home page, where there were some core word options. I tried modeling both "go" and "more" after hitting pause. He was more receptive to "more," since he had prior experience with people prompting him to ask for "more."

Throughout the session, I tried to "push the envelope." I modeled "more + Thomas," "more + watch," "more + DVD," "want + watch," "want + more," and "want + Thomas." He was most stimulable for 2-

button sequences that didn't require navigating, so "more" and "want + more" were the easiest for him to follow and attempt. "Want + watch" also got some responses near the end of the session, as watch was on the home page of one of the displays. I also modeled "like" and "funny" at times and, when it looked like he was getting restless, I modeled "different" and "all done," to see if he wanted to watch a different DVD or just wanted out of there. When I hit "all done" he immediately got up and went over to his mother. He understood, but did not yet express that message.

There are a couple of points in this snapshot. One is that I chose an activity I knew would interest him and hold his attention. Watching a movie together may not always be the most interactive activity, but it is a place to start. Secondly, I noted his ability to use single word responses, to use words with which he was more familiar and had been prompted to use before, and to be stimulable for use of basic 2 core word sequences.

What should be done within the assessment is to push the Zone of Proximal Development. (ZPD) The zone of proximal development, a concept introduced by Lev Vygotsky in the 1930's, is the difference between what an individual can do without help and what he can do with support. Vygotsky believed that when learning was properly organized cognitive development ensued. Applying learning strategies to an individual set in motion development that occurs only when the child is interacting with others in the environment. He believed that individuals play an important active role in learning.

So, during the brief time you have in an assessment, your job is to begin to define the limits of that zone. If he used 1 word, can you get him to use 2? If he only used the page displayed, can he navigate from that page to 1 other? How about 2? If he used 1 core word, can I get him to add another?

Model, Pause, Prompt, Pause Again.

ASSESSMENT SNAPSHOT

L.D. was a 17-year-old girl with cerebral palsy. She had had very limited experience with AAC because she could not access the paper-based displays used in class. Her teacher and SLP held up 2 choices of items or pictures for her to choose, but had not tried larger arrays or other access modes.

L.D. came into the initial background session with her hair done nicely, wearing jewelry and a little lipstick. She was reported to be a "typical teenager," with preferences for clothing and accessories. She enjoyed talking about teen heartthrobs and musicians.

When she came back for the assessment, I had a variety of songs on my iPad and a tray of nail polish and eye shadow, in addition to my usual bag of "stuff." Her eyes went straight to the nail polish. During the assessment we tried a variety of scanning patterns and switches for access, as well as eye gaze technology. We looked at switch placement, array size, and type of symbol used. We checked for color preference for buttons and backgrounds, as well as placement because her vision was unknown.

She and I "chatted" while I did her nails. I modeled making comments about the colors, the job I was doing, and the music she chose for use to listen to. By the time I was done with her nails (I am notoriously slow at these things in evaluations), we had helped her gain some understanding of how the scanning worked and when to hit the switch. When I helped her get to a "chat" page, she was able to make comments; something she had never been able to do before, but something she was clearly able to do given the tools.

The point of this snapshot is a big one - never underestimate the individual. This young lady clearly had things she wanted to say, and the language skills to say them when provided with an AAC system with the vocabulary to do so.

Sometimes you will find an individual who has no play skills, nothing in particular he likes to do, nothing you - or his team members - can find to motivate him. At these times, the most motivating messages can be "Leave me alone," "I need a break," "Do different," "Stop." Model those, then honor them. No matter how "uncommunicative" the individual appears to be, he has some behaviors he uses to communicate. Find those, find the message behind them, and develop a plan to replace them with the appropriate communication mode.

I once spent about 40 minutes wandering around the house with Sam, a young man (about 30) with autism. I followed him from room to room as he tried to get away from me, and my request that he communicate with me more efficiently. He had had high-tech AAC systems in the past, but was no longer using them, in part due to increasing loss of vision. After several times telling him that if he wanted me to leave him alone he would have to tell me, he finally reached out to the dynamic display device I was carrying, found the "Leave me alone" message and used it. I left him alone. At the least, I knew he was capable of using an AAC system when it really mattered to him.

Communication functions were mentioned above and are an important part of an AAC assessment - or any language assessment for an individual with significant language needs.

Equipment for Assessments

Not many SLPs are fortunate to have an AAC clinic or lab available in which to do assessments with a wide array of available technology. At the least, there should be an array of paper-based displays available including PODD communication books, core vocabulary books and displays, different types of switches and alternate access technology as needed, and an array of dynamic display technology.

It is this last requirement that is difficult for many SLPs. One solution is to use your local manufacturer's representatives – that is what they are there for. Ask to borrow devices or have them bring them. Alternatively, find out if there are loan programs in your area. Several states have state funded programs from which SLPs, families and users can borrow a range of technology.

While nothing is going to take the place of device matching trials in AAC, single practitioners and school-based speech-language pathologists with limited equipment budgets can make the most of the new iOS technology and the proliferation of AAC, fine motor, and language-based apps when performing AAC evaluations.

The explosion of these apps provides a wealth of data mining opportunities for evaluators. Using them to gather much of the information needed in many AAC assessments means less emphasis on having a complete range of AAC devices on hand - something only some evaluation centers have the "luxury" of providing.

While many of the AAC apps available are simple choice boards and offer minimal ability to expand and really teach or use language, there are others that have lots of potential as assessment tools, even if not sufficiently robust as a primary AAC tool. Judiciously budgeting for a small number of these can provide a wide range of assessment tools for private practitioners and schools.

Once again: we want to define the individual's skills and abilities in language (both current and extended possible;) physical abilities in vision, hearing, physical access modality; response to environmental demands, barriers, and partner skills.

1. What is the individual doing now; what more could they do given changes in partner training, changes in the encoding system, changes in the access mode, etc.?

2. What features does an AAC system for this individual need to have - voice type, screen size, array size, encoding method and then icon type or literacy limits?

All of the answers need to come from the process of evaluating this individual with the best tools we can obtain benefit.

CHAPTER 5
Intervention

*1. Choose, *2. Plan, *3. Prepare, *4. Implement

Communicative competence was defined by Janice Light (1989) as: "– the state of being functionally adequate in daily communication and of having sufficient knowledge, judgment, and skills to communicate effectively in daily life."

I am advocating a 4-step process to building AAC use: Choose, Plan, Prepare, and Implement.

Step 1: Choosing vocabulary was discussed in Chapter 3, as we talked about core and fringe vocabulary words, preprogramed phrases, and categorical and pragmatic vocabulary arrangements.

Step 2: Once you have the vocabulary set in your AAC system, you want to plan your intervention strategy. Think about what words you want to target first. Are you going to target 1 word at a time (as in the Word of the Week strategy*) or 12 words per month (as presented on the PrAACticalAAC blog's Year of Core Words*?)

Are you going to focus on core words used in a single activity or those identified core words whenever they occur in the environment naturally?

When you have decided your targets, then use a planning system/template (some are provided in the Appendix) to plan what you are going to say, which core words you will target, how and when you are going to model, (single words? phrases?)

Step 3: Next, prepare. Prepare with a modeling plan, as above, and the materials you need for whatever activity you are going to use each step of the way. Become comfortable with the child's AAC system sufficiently to be able to model the words you have set as targets. This is important. You might even want to practice ahead of time. But don't worry if you make mistakes or have to stop and think about where a word is. These are perfect times to use verbal referencing and talk about what you are doing.

Use of "verbal referencing" - talking to the individual about what is happening while the partner searches for a symbol or navigates to a page to find a desired word and explaining how (x-word) can be used in in (y) context - demonstrates the process and the strategies, helps with the individual's understanding of others' messages, and provides models for their own expression.

Partners should use pictures while talking, producing messages for a wide variety of communicative functions (e.g. questions, comments, greetings, requests, responses, giving and asking for information, telling, directing), using as much of the available vocabulary as is possible/practical. Using aided language for commands or questions should be minimized; maximize use of statements and comments. In order to do this, partners must be familiar with the location of vocabulary in the system. They should practice with other partners to get comfortable with it.

Verbal referencing gives a concise talking through the process of finding the word. These times provide examples of how to get to the words you want when you're unsure, and let children know you're learning, too.

To prepare, you need to think about the activity, think about the target language skill, and plan what support is needed for the student to meet the target. Or, rather than form (grammar, syntax, morphology, length of utterance), you might think about function. (the type of communication intent) What type of message does the student need? Plan for when that context happens. What should the student say? How can you incorporate that target?

Step 4: Implement. That is our focus in this chapter. But first, some background information:

If you can stand reading about statistics, here are a few from different studies:

von Tetzchner (1997) and Porter (2009) both refer to the differences in language environments between typically developing children and AAC users. Children are typically surrounded by examples of others using the communication systems they are learning. Hart and Risely (1995) found that typical children in working class families hear approximately 1,250 words per hour and accumulate a listening vocabulary of 6 million words by the time they are 3 years old. They also reported (1995) that 4-year-olds from working-class families and families on welfare had considerably smaller vocabularies than their age-mates from professional families. This difference has been called the "30-Million-Word Gap" and "The Great Catastrophe."

The average 3-year-old in a middle-class household hears about 6 million words per year. The average deaf child the same age and background (and in a signing home) sees approximately the same number of signs. But the average nonverbal 3-year-old sees 0 instances of someone using pictures to communicate.

According to von Tetzchner (1997) "the difference between their own expressive (and for some also receptive) language and the language used by significant people in their immediate surroundings" is a critical factor in the acquisition of language for AAC users. There is an assumption in all major theories of language learning that the individual is surrounded by others in the environment using the same language system.

Even in second language learning the importance of immersion has been noted. Learners of second languages need to participate in an environment that exposes them to - immerses them in - experiences with that language in order to become competent communicators. Parents and others engage often in routines with children that demonstrate how the world is organized, what words people use in those organized routines, what people's roles are in routines, (who says what when) and how to interact with others in these routines; even before they can participate in the conversation.

"The average 18-month-old child has been exposed to 4,380 hours of oral language at the rate of 8 hours/day from birth. A child who has a communication system and receives speech/language therapy two times per week for 20-30-minute sessions will reach this same amount of language exposure in 84 years." (Jane Korsten 2011).

Because this type of immersion environment is rarely provided (although beginning to find foothold) to learners of AAC, there is a great discrepancy for them between the language environment to which they are exposed, which uses verbal language, and the language system they are being asked to use, which is a picture-based language.

In order to achieve communicative competence, the AAC user must be provided with maximized language input in the same mode he is going to be using. Therefore, we need to model use of the system, to show how it can be used successfully, for a variety of messages, for all communication needs.

We need to use the system to communicate TO the student and use the same system to MODEL for the student how to say what one wants to say in a variety of contexts. We are not just teaching which symbol means what word, we're providing a genuine purpose for using the symbol. This process of modeling the AAC system's use is called Aided Language Stimulation. It is also sometimes referred to as Aided Input, Natural Aided Language or Partner Aided Input. As I said in Chapter 2, I'm using Aided Language Stimulation as an umbrella term in this book.

Aided Language Stimulation is the strategy by which the communication partner (usually an adult) models using the AAC system when speaking to the child; using the pictures in conjunction with speaking to interact for genuine purposes in real contexts, demonstrating when and how to use specific vocabulary in natural contexts.

The objective is to try to balance out the discrepancy in language systems that the individual experiences and is learning to use. Aided Language Stimulation usually involves the use of the same system the student is using. This can be dependent upon how much "ownership" the child has of his communication system. Some students will not let others use their communication system; it is, after all, their voice. PODD books have a "Group PODD" that can be used by the teacher. While the system components are the same and the operational guidelines are the same, there may be differences in the number of symbols per page or the availability of specific symbols based on the specific AAC users in the classroom.

This is the first step in all AAC intervention with children. This is the input that typical children get through our talking to and around them. This is the input that AAC users need to develop those same language skills in their mode of communication.

It is used in order to:

> increase the child's exposure to a variety of vocabulary, across different communicative functions, in genuine, natural contexts,

> increase the child's comprehension of language concepts with clear structure; establishing associations,

> provide a format for all communication partners to learn the concept of modeling (as well as to become familiar with the AAC system).

We:

1. Identify potential target vocabulary within specified activities/contexts.

2. Select vocabulary to target.

3. Provide Aided Language Stimulation (ALgS)/ modeling. The AAC system needs to be available during the targeted activities. Ideally, it should/needs to be available at all times. Make sure the communication partner(s) know(s) the intended target words. The partner will model each of the words, showing the child how the word is used in that context and where to find it in the AAC system. Initially, we do not expect the child to use the word/symbol. Make sure the child can see the AAC system and observe the modeling process. If there is voice output, you might want to turn the volume down so that the child is listening primarily to the partner. Be careful not to give directions, test, or make the child perform. Don't ask the child to "Show me _" or "What is _?" or "Where is _?" Remember that communication for real purposes and messages is the goal, not trying to find out how much the child knows.

4. Use expectant pauses and natural cues. At the point when the partner would begin modeling, stop and insert an expectant pause. Give an expectant look with associated gestures (tilting of head, raising of eyebrows, etc).. Wait a couple seconds to see what the child does. If the child reaches to the AAC system and touches the target the partner should say the word and carry through with the activity. If the child reaches to the AAC system but misses the target slightly, respond as if the child was accurate, and provide an accurate model. If the child does not reach to the target, wait briefly to see if he does something that can be regarded as an initiation of communication. Whether or not he does, model the target word and carry through with the activity.

5. Collect data.

It is very difficult to provide such aided input when the AAC system is largely comprised of whole phrase messages and in a low-tech system. The range of vocabulary available in these systems in minimal, and not nearly sufficient to provide input throughout multiple environments and contexts. The system's limited availability of visual space restricts the number of words that can be used at any given time. When the number of symbols per page is further restricted by difficulties with visual or motor access, it becomes impossible to use such a system to provide models of picture communication use.

The aim of Aided Language Stimulation (ALgS) is to create an aided language learning environment that models interactive use of the AAC system by others in the user's daily environment. ALgS teaches language to AAC users in the same way that language is taught to typically developing children. It also teaches the user how to think about language which is important.

To this end, those interacting with the user need to use the user's communication system - or a similar system - when they communicate to him, as well as use the system to MODEL to the user how to say what they want or need to say with the system in a variety of contexts. The teaching environment needs to create more of a balance between what the user hears/sees used in the environment and what he is expected to use to communicate.

Talk to the user while using their communication system to communicate to them. Highlight key words and provide a model that is linguistically one step beyond how the user is communicating. This goes beyond teaching which symbol means which word, which has been found to be relatively worthless for communicating. Aided language environments provide genuine purpose for the symbol(s).

Partners should give users feedback on the effectiveness of their communication attempts, and provide message expansion. Also provide recasts; a modification by the communication partners of the user's response that corrects an error or provides the next linguistic step.

Partners should ask themselves: "Am I modeling a range of different communication intents? Am I modeling different types of messages? Am I modeling using the system to interact, have a conversation? Am I modeling strategies for when I make a mistake, or the other person doesn't understand me?"

The end result is that the individual's knowledge of the vocabulary and of language skills will increase. There should be increased mean length of utterance (use of longer phrases or sentences), better syntactic skills, and more varied use of communication functions.

Comprehension and expression are promoted through this use of models during motivating and frequently occurring activities and routines. ALgS attempts to provide the same kind of language learning environment that is available to verbal children for children who use aided symbols. These children need to see models of their system being used interactively by others who are communicating real messages in real situations, they need to have multiple opportunities to practice using their system to communicate real messages in real situations while being provided with the appropriate level of scaffolding required to be successful, they need to receive natural feedback, and they need to have their messages expanded by others using the same mode of communication they use, so that they can learn to communicate more effectively.

ALgS requires that the needed symbol vocabulary is available in the environment at all times, that the aided symbols are used for genuine communication throughout the day, and that partners are trained to use the aided symbol systems competently.

Aided language systems include use of visual symbols for expression, use of visual symbols for comprehension and conjunction with speech, and use of visual symbols to represent the organization of an activity, script or schedule. The key to aided language systems is the consistent use of symbols for two-way communication by all communication partners in all environments.

Aided language can take a little practice to become comfortable with using at the outset, but it is crucial to the individual learning to use his AAC system. In the process, communication partners begin to get a feeling for what challenges the user faces.

Significant information about how to use ALgS is provided to users of the PODD communication books. PODD developer Gayle Porter insists that use of ALgS is at least as integral a part of the AAC process as determining the functions and vocabulary the system contains. Discussions of ALgS have been in the literature for many years (Goosens, Crain, &Elder 1992, Romski & Sevcik 1996, Cafiero 1998, Bruno, Bruno and Trembath 2006, Mirenda 2009). Research for its use dates to the 1990's and it is evidence-based practice for AAC learning.

Porter breaks communication partners down into groups: those who need the skills to understand the user's communication, the skills to provide ALgS consistently, and the ability to teach communication skills are the first and most important group. These are the individual's key communication partners, and the ones who need to learn most specifically the individual's communication responses and be most familiar with the AAC system. These are the users who will be prominent in providing aided language input.

The second group is comprised of those who need only the skills to operate the system in order to understand the user's communication attempts. This is a significant distinction for the purpose of training.

Bronfenbrenner's (2006) ecological model puts the individual in the center of an ever-widening group of influences; including people and environments. Focusing on the individual includes identifying his strengths, skills, needs, and success with AAC. Linguistic, cognitive, motor, sensory status are all evaluated.

But focusing on this information alone is not enough to predict future success with AAC. The individual does not exist in a vacuum. Rather, he lives in a wider context, with an environment that responds - or doesn't - to him in a variety of ways. Consider the availability of an AAC system in his environment, as well as the opportunities for communicating with the system. Finally, in the broadest sense, consider how people in his society view an AAC user; how much acceptance is there? How much is he included or excluded socially?

All partners who are using aided language modeling need to remember that - at some stage - once they provide a model of a target language concept they need to wait and to signal to the user that they are waiting for a response. The "expectant look" has come to be the accepted term for this signal. This can be manifested by the cocked head, raised eye brow, wide eyes, and even shrugged shoulders. It lets the individual know that their communication partner is waiting for them to take their turn.

If there is no response from the AAC user, the partner should know the procedure for prompting a turn. It is important to use this strategy in the most naturalistic communication exchanges possible, and not just for asking and answering questions. The AAC user needs to learn that communication is not always about "testing" whether or not they can answer the question, but about taking turns to exchange messages. The more the AAC user learns to respond to a signal of expectation rather than a specific question, the more natural the communication exchange becomes - it becomes a conversation.

Aided language systems include use of visual symbols for expression, use of visual symbols for comprehension in conjunction with speech, and use of visual symbols to represent the organization of an activity, script or schedule. The key to aided language systems is the consistent use of symbols for two-way communication by all communication partners in all environments.

The biggest predictor of a child's success in school is his vocabulary. (Remember that '30 million word' gap?) Some parents just have a better idea of what to say and do, especially when reading to their children. They know their child needs to hear words repeated over and over again in meaningful sentences and questions. (Hart & Risely, 1975). So, what's so key about routines?

Well, these are often the times when parents speak the most to their children. And what they say is often repeated over and over again, using the same words and in the same order every time. This repetition and predictability help their children build their vocabulary and their schema for how their life is organized.

Research tells us that routines are the heart of symbol and language development. Routines are sequences of actions or events that are repeated over and over regularly. Each routine can be broken down into smaller and smaller components. Each of these components is influenced by the responses and reactions of those involved. The reactions and responses become symbols that are used in those interactions to signal to each other. [Remember, symbols are signals that are interpreted the same way by at least 2 people.] When the routine always follows the same sequence, the signals between the two people involved become shared symbols. Routines help us build symbolic awareness, and symbols become communicative when they come to have a more standardized or conventional meaning in a larger group. This helps us realize why it is important to develop routines in thinking about intervention for AAC (Lonke, 2014) and for understanding the impact of Aided Language Stimulation   Break routines down into their smaller component steps. Help to ensure that the child understands the sequence of the routine. And say the same things every time at every step. In this way, the child becomes familiar with the words you use.

Be flexible. Follow the child's lead, but rather than denying him some off-topic or off-sequence behavior, make it a contingency that he do what is involved in the routine in order to gain access to what he wanted to do.

Make sure to use appropriate language to label or describe what catches the child's interest, as well as what is involved in the routine. By naming and describing what caught the child's interest, you provide input of vocabulary that is motivating.

Think outside the box. While we want the child to learn the structure and attending language of the routine, we also want to take advantage of those moments when the child's interest is piqued by something else in the environment.

Also consider that a routine can be made out of any repeated activity. Think about the things that the child and caregiver do together. No matter how small or extended, a routine can be a pivotal part of the child's language intervention. So, if you're looking for ways to begin to implement core vocabulary with your AAC user, you need look no further than the everyday routines.

The opportunity to be immersed in an environment using aided language is very rare. For AAC users and learners, there is little if any opportunity to even observe others using an AAC system, let alone be immersed in an environment of AAC users. But without this, children learning to use AAC systems constantly need to figure out how to use a language system they have rarely - or never - seen used to communicate. Not having models of others using aided language results in the student not knowing how to use a language system they have never seen used.

Once use of Aided Language Stimulation has been established to introduce word use to the individual, explicit teaching activities need to be implemented to teach new words. Facilitators need to teach explicitly, then elaborate on the meaning and use of the word through a variety of meaningful activities. The AAC user needs to be exposed to the word repeatedly and consistently.

Choice making is an early language opportunity that is already, or can be easily, built into daily activities and routines. Offering students choices of what is done, where and when it is done, and/or with whom can provide students with opportunities to exert control over their environment and learn about the usefulness of communicating.

By taking a look at how the classroom or home day unfolds, we can create simple scripts for routines that help build communication by providing communication partners with the vocabulary needed for each step within the routine for a variety of communication functions.

Every classroom day begins with students arriving or, in a more structured activity, specific greetings and acknowledgement during circle time or morning meeting. This is an opportunity for students to learn greetings exchanges, make comments, express feelings, and learn names.

Every student's school day has at least 1 mealtime, and often students also have breakfast and/or snack at school. Again, this is a daily routine with specific actions and opportunities. And eating is often a reinforcing activity for students. Students can express choices, make requests, protest, comment, express opinions, ask for help. Students who purchase lunch have more natural opportunities for communication than students who bring their meal, but either way staff can provide opportunities for talking about not just the meal, but how the student feels about it, what he likes or doesn't, and what he is going to do at the break time that typically comes after lunch.

Additionally, students typically wash their hands before lunch and often after it, as well. Staff can provide input in the form of directions and can sabotage the process by moving the soap or towels out of reach sometimes; so that students need to ask for help. Describing words, like clean and dirty, can be modeled, as well as the vocabulary for each step in the sequence.

So, to recap, it is easy to implement AAC in the classroom by

1. offering choices as often as possible

2. using consistent vocabulary and sequences within frequently repeated classroom routines

3. sabotaging the environment during a routine task so that students need to communicate

4. utilize simple scripts within routines so that staff are consistently modeling the same vocabulary and sentence types

5. make sure to model vocabulary used during routines that goes beyond requesting; to include commenting, providing information, asking questions, and other communication functions

AAC implementation does not need to take a significant amount of planning time or equipment. Just think about the language you use **routinely**.

In one class I worked with a few years ago there were students with a variety of Complex Communication Needs, sensory needs, and medical needs. There was not a lot of AAC going on, but the teacher was eager to learn. Here are a few of the things she instituted:

1. At circle time, the teacher used a Big Mack button to have students respond to taking attendance. Access was an issue for many of the students. So, where the BigMack button was held was a big issue. And this was just 1 single response.

2. One of the students had the motor skills to touch a target with her hand independently, and the ability to use more words. I made her a PODD book, and demonstrated how to provide Aided Language Stimulation consistently. I provided support monthly throughout the school year.

3. At one point, this student needed to have something that was more compact. Aides were having a difficult time dealing with her behavior in the room, which included trying to contain flailing arms and legs and head butts.

    So, since they told me they couldn't handle the PODD book, and I wanted to make sure whatever AAC I was providing was getting used consistently, I backpedaled and went to a small (20 symbol) core word board, with some activity specific fringe words (presented in pages of 6 symbols) for the 2-3 favored activities she would spend some time in.

    This student had some cortical vision issues, so these symbols were printed with bright red and yellow borders and high-contrast symbols where available.

4. For other students, I looked at adapting books and encouraged the teacher to do more read-alouds and shared reading with specific objectives in mind. For the students in this class who were going

to be involved in shared reading activities, she needed a way for them to respond to questions or make comments. For most, this involved using eye gaze.

So, we went from the teacher holding up a 2-choice array to a version of an eye gaze board with 4 choices, and then 8. Thus, student response choices were quadrupled in a short period of time. And, with multiple boards with this many choices, there was a bigger array of responses possible.

5. Speaking of read aloud time, this was another opportunity to use the Big Mac buttons or a Sequencer. Recording the repeated line of text gives students a way to participate. Recording sequential lines gives them even more opportunities.

6. Access was the biggest problem with this group of students. She added visual cues and communication opportunities in as many places as possible. We looked at a variety of different switches for them to use and I pushed Partner Assisted Scanning as a no-tech mode. (District purchasing processes are still a mystery to me. All I know is it usually takes forever. In this case I was happily surprised).

We looked at SCATiR switches, toggle switches, sip-n-puff, pillow switches, and more. Fortunately, we also had access to the California Assistive Technology Exchange (CATE) loan program. This allowed trials of a wider variety of switches than we would have had access to. Many states have such programs now, so check for such resources in your state or city.

7. I made large, 3X5 card sized symbols so that there was a classroom sized communication board that was core word based, that was large enough for all the students (with the exception of those totally blind) to see, that was high contrast for students with vision disorders, and whose symbols were easily removed one at a time during instruction time to emphasize use of the target core word. Any opportunity to use a core word is important.

Access to symbols needs to be as easy as possible. Putting these cards into a large pocket chart provided that quick and easy access to enough core words that the teacher could use them seamlessly in instruction.

Using aided input during routines is a great way to introduce the core vocabulary in consistent formats. With this particular group of students, life was full of routines. Between changing diapers and clothes, washing up, feeding (which for a number of them was via G-tube), and other daily care routines there were a lot of times throughout the day when the same sequence was carried out and talked through. Perfect opportunities to provide aided language.

What kind of core words can you use?

Diaper changing: off, on, clean, dirty, up, wipe, wet, dry

Feeding: open, close, more, stop, different, like, not like, go, away, mine

Greetings: hi, me, yes, no, good, not

I'll have more suggestions coming up. And note that all of these example can be found at home, as well.

Communication intervention needs to be as functional as possible, rather than removed from real-life contexts.

Functional communication with an AAC system can include making choices, making requests, responding to personal questions, asking questions of others, stating your needs, commenting on some experience, and more.

Therapeutic activities, on the other hand, are those that improve a specific communication skill. Sometimes it is necessary to practice these skills removed from their usual, natural context, or in contexts that are engineered to provide an opportunity to practice the skill with support/scaffolding, feedback, modeling. In therapeutic activities the SLP practices with the AAC user using specific vocabulary to describe or give directions, learning how to sequence steps to a task or the order of events in a day.

For AAC users to become competent communicators, they need both functional and therapeutic activities. They need to learn how to use their AAC systems to communicate with others effectively and efficiently. They also need the same kind of practice in specific language skills that we provide to other students with language delays and disorders. And for many of these activities, there is no difference in the content for AAC users, only in the mode of how materials are presented how the individual responds to them.

As SLPs in our brief structured intervention time (which is never sufficient but all that can happen, often because of caseload sizes), we need to focus on both functional and therapeutic intervention.

AAC users need both of these types of intervention activities in order to learn how to use the AAC system and become competent communicators. They need to learn specific language structures and can use many of the same therapeutic activities as other students; only the mode of response changes.

We need to recognize that AAC users often do not get the same opportunities to practice morphology and syntax, do not get the same opportunities to practice vocabulary as their peers.

We need to remember to keep intervention activities fun, novel, and student-centered. Giving students the opportunity and power to control aspects of the situation shows them the power of communication.

This can work at home, as well as therapy times. Children can have the options to choose what activities to do, what order in which to do them, the pace of the activity, and the ability to express booth negative and positive opinions.

Use the child's own interests. Use of meaningful activities that revolve around his interests will maximize motivation.

Do something novel or unexpected. This captures attention quickly. Most importantly, teach language in context; in real, meaningful interactions, as much as possible.

Do not think you can teach language in discrete trial drill formats. A study (Berkowitz, 1988, 1989) showed that symbol meanings and discriminations taught in discrete trial format did not result in students using those symbols once they were placed in their communication books. It was not until the symbols were taught in context, with modified incidental teaching strategies, that students used them appropriately.

You can build skills and develop vocabulary in therapeutic activities, but you must develop language in natural contexts. This is where the partnership becomes critical. Students need that carry-over between therapeutic contexts and natural contexts in order to "own" the vocabulary we're teaching. Parents and professionals need to be partners in this process.

Whatever the environment you are in, you need to think about the activity you want to engage the child with, think about the language skills you are targeting, and plan what support is needed for the student to achieve this target.

Language intervention techniques that increase early expressive communication skills include Aided AAC Modeling, Expectant Delay, Open-Ended Wh-Questions, Brief Verbal Prompting, and Increased Responsivity.

The over-reaching expectation of all of AAC intervention needs to be the idea and belief that the individual has something to say. It is our job to figure out what that is.

The research shows that teaching words with a variety of uses and functions for communicating is important for AAC users to become effective communicators. But what is the first thing we teach children with complex communication needs? Nouns. The focus is often on meeting basic wants and needs, or avoiding behavioral problems by providing what the child wants to ask for. However, a close look at the child's environment shows that, for the most part, basic needs and wants are met, and caregivers know what the child wants when it is a concrete or preferred item or activity. As a result, the AAC user ends up being able to label items without being able to tell whether he likes them or not, wants them or not, has a problem with them or not, needs them moved, wants something different instead of them, or had one of them yesterday.

The second thing we often teach children with complex communication needs is specific sentence structures, whole message units, and specific carrier phrases. The result is that they have little opportunity to learn language structures, little opportunity for spontaneous generation of novel utterances (SNUG), little opportunity to project their own intent upon messages, and that they have artificial sounding speech or voice output.

Some of the first phrases taught to AAC users are "I want," and "I see." But how about "I don't want," "Go away," "Leave me alone," "Something different," "I need a break," "Need help," "He's bugging me," "Want to go," or "It mine."

Students with complex communication needs need a sufficiently robust communication system to be able to communicate all of their needs, all of the time. Building that AAC system and teaching them how to use those words is the biggest component of AAC.

Effective intervention is providing structured opportunities to communicate, providing these opportunities over and over again, providing these opportunities in multiple contexts, and providing sufficient vocabulary to make these opportunities meaningful.

Students with significant communication needs must receive numerous and highly structured opportunities. Research tells us 200 opportunities per day. Incidental learning opportunities are not always effective for acquisition of new forms. There are, of course, exceptions to the rule; but these tend to be students whose potential for language acquisition was severely underestimated.

The communication demands of each type of interaction are significantly different. The AAC user/learner needs to learn and develop the skills needed to meet these demands while simultaneously learning language and learning to operate the AAC system.

The development of communication competence is also very strongly influenced by the barriers and supports in the individuals' environments. Supports must be sufficient to overcome the barriers. In all cases the barriers must be identified and removed, either through direct intervention with the individual, or with changes to the environment or partners.

So, having previously learned the different types of options available, and now how to provide modeling, what do you do?

In general, we need to teach 4 different competencies to AAC users: basic operational skills, linguistic competencies, social competencies, and literacy competencies. (Light 1989)

We often tend to focus on linguistic competency first and foremost, but often don't get beyond requesting. Operational and literacy competencies tend to be the least important concerns for communication partners, unfortunately. This is a good time to take a look at the AAC Profile, developed by Tracy Kovachs and sold by Linguisystems if you're a SLP. This checklist offers not just a structure for figuring out where a student is along these 4 competencies, but also provides a roadmap for our objectives for the student.

For parents, it is a helpful view of structuring their child's skills and needs in a more specific manner than we often can give them.

AAC users' development of linguistic, operational and social competencies are all impacted by the limitations of their various disorders, and by the limitations of the AAC system itself. Despite intervention, AAC users may be restricted by the limits of what the AAC system can provide for them. A child who is not literate yet, for example, is dependent upon others to provide vocabulary for him to use and may often find situations in which he does not have the word that he needs for the context. A severely involved individual with cerebral palsy or muscular dystrophy may be reliant on switch scanning access to the AAC system, and therefore not be able to maintain the speed of interaction in typical conversational exchanges.

In these and other instances the AAC user will need to develop strategies to optimize efficient and effective communication with the limits of the system itself. Strategic competence can allow the AAC user to attain communicative competence in spite of the linguistic, operational, or social impairments.

Strategic Competency is unique to AAC and refers to the understanding and use of those skills needed to facilitate communication; such as getting the partner's attention before using a symbol, using a different word/message/strategy if the partner does not understand, knowing what to say in a given situation.

Linguistic Competency refers to receptive and expressive language skills; including vocabulary use and word relationships, comprehension and use of syntax, and grammar, etc.

Social Competency refers to those social skills needed in communicating; such as asking and answering questions, using and following up greetings, repairing communication breakdowns, providing information and opinions.

Operational Skills refers to the skills required to use the AAC system or device. This includes powering the device on and off, opening the communication book to the correct page, navigating between pages, going back to the last page, etc.

Using Operational Speech - talking about what to do with the system to get to the word or message wanted - allows them to hear what the process is, and begin to understand the operational system.

Comprehension and expression are promoted through this use of models during motivating and frequently occurring activities and routines. ALgS attempts to provide the same kind of language learning environment that is available to verbal children for children who use aided symbols. These children need to see models of their system being used interactively by others who are communicating real messages in real situations, they need to have multiple opportunities to practice using their system to communicate real messages in real situations while being provided with the appropriate level of scaffolding required to be successful, they need to receive natural feedback, and they need to have their messages expanded by others using the same mode of communication they use, so that they can learn to communicate more effectively.

Linguistic competency is usually our first priority, but often only to a limited extent. There is a tendency to focus on labeling and requesting; both of which are fairly "dead end" functions. And too often, AAC users are not taught specific syntax or morphology or a wide range of communication functions. I will attempt to give you, here, some ideas for reaching those areas

Building Core Word Use

A little review first. Oftentimes AAC users are first taught to recognize and use pictures or symbols for concrete objects, as I've said before. The assumption, in part, is that concrete items will be more easily understood by, and therefore used by, the beginning AAC user. However, nouns have relatively little use outside of requesting which, in itself, is a "dead end" communication function, as mentioned previously. Once a request for an item has been made there is little - or nothing - else to say. Nouns by themselves convey no meaning except as labels, and rarely tell the communicative intent of the user beyond the possibility of requesting.

Core vocabulary, on the other hand, is re-useable vocabulary, and consists of high frequency words that are used over and over in multiple contexts and with clear meaning. Core words may take more direct instruction and time to learn, but once learned can be used in multiple ways across multiple situations.

Symbols for core vocabulary are more abstract than nouns. Verbs may be understood from a symbol, as well as some adjectives and spatial concepts. But many core words are not transparent to the "listener" without reading the label positioned above them. Using context in teaching these words, then, becomes even more important. Real, authentic experiences in which the word is used will teach the word and its symbol, regardless of the opacity of the symbol itself.

Regardless of whether core words will be built one at a time or a dozen at a time, it is important to start with a display that is larger than the beginning point, that is approximately a size that will be functional for the individual for a while. Often 25-36 location grids are used as a starting point. Sometimes larger grids are used.

The grid can have just a single word/symbol, or a few, to begin with, with more core words added as language and communication grow. What is important about this concept is that the vocabulary be placed in its permanent location from the beginning, so that it remains stable throughout learning. This stability of location helps students to learn through motor planning and allows many of our students, who use only peripheral vision most of the time, can find a button they want without having to look too carefully. (insert figure of 3 versions of the same board as words are added)

As new words are added, emphasize that new word more than others in Aided Language Input and elicitation strategies. Provide activities that focus on that word more than others, while still maintaining use of words that have been established. Beyond contextual use, begin to add practice activities that practice locating and using the word in decontextual activities. Modify traditional games so that the words needed to play them are the words you've been building. For students who can't draw to illustrate the meaning of a word - a key vocabulary building activity - cut out pictures from magazines and old books. Have the individual decide if the picture "goes with" (represents or is associated with) the core word or not. Much like Word Walls are used in literacy instruction, Zangari (2013) suggests creating a Core Word Wall with the core words that have been learned. Keep adding to it. You can make this out of a tri-fold science fair display or manila file folders glued together.

While much of our early intervention focuses on an initial - or universal* - core vocabulary set, we need to think beyond this initial set of core words. Once our students/children have gained consistent access to these initial core words, we need to add more specialized core words for enhanced message building and increased syntax. And once students move beyond initial and expanded core words, then we need to add individualized core words, as well as more fringe.

SLPs spend relatively little time in the classroom or even in therapy with the student. Therefore, the training of teachers, paraprofessionals and parents is critical. While SLPs can get the team started, ultimately success is out of their hands. Parents and classroom staff spend far more time with the child, and have far more opportunities to build core and academic language.

Initial core words are more universal, and are used for a variety of functions for which there are multiple opportunities across multiple topics. Use of more individualized and specialized core words may be restricted to specific topics or situations. These words may only have opportunities for practice in the context of specific activities or curricular content.

Universal Core: universal core is terminology used by the Developmental Learning Maps (DLM), determined by review of literature, CCSS, and frequency of appearance in written text. (Erickson, UNC-Chapel Hill)

Like, want, get, make, good, more

Not, go, look, turn, help, different

I, he, open, do, put, same

You, she, that, up, all, some

It, here, in, on, can, finished

Where, what, why, who, when, stop

Teaching in Context with Active Participation

Everything we know about learning theory suggests that contextualized teaching is best for typical and special learners alike. While typical individuals learn through decontextualized activities more and more as they progress through school and through life, many AAC users continue to rely upon contextualized learning far longer. While we must provide decontextualized practice and generalized experiences, initially the AAC user will learn most successfully within the context in which they will need or want to use the word.

Providing word learning through use in context actually strengthens generalization. By providing opportunities to use the word in a context that the individual will want or need to use it, the chances are increased that he will be able to use it when the opportunity or need arises.

For some learners, such as those with Autism Spectrum Disorder or developmental disabilities, the need to provide word learning in context is even stronger. These are learners who will not successfully learn to use words functionally out of context. For these learners, especially, learning by doing - active participation - is crucial.

Teaching vocabulary to any individual in any context requires using a variety of multimodal strategies. Evidence based vocabulary instruction (Marzano) involves interacting with the new word in a variety of ways, including defining, illustrating, using in context, explaining through words or pictures, creating art or music that defines or describes the word, and discussing the word with others.

Many of these strategies are obviated by the fact that the learner is nonverbal and may not have sufficient vocabulary in his own lexicon to describe or define other words; particularly core words. The AAC user may also have physical or motor limitations that restricts ability to draw, paint, or create nonverbal representations independently. For the AAC learner the word is more often used in context initially to provide definition, rather than writing a definition or sentence. But many of the classroom and intervention strategies used for all learners can be used with those beginning communicators using AAC.

It is important to build a variety of contexts for using the new word in the classroom or intervention environment. Create thematic lessons. Have a theme of the week or the month. Find ways to use the new words in activities that revolve around the theme. Thematic instruction has many advantages for students with language difficulties; including the fact that keeping the content vocabulary consistent over a period of time provides more opportunities to learn that vocabulary as well as the specific word(s) being targeted. It allows the learner to focus less on a constantly shifting array of content vocabulary from multiple themes or topics, and focus more on the communication word(s) to be learned. Themes are often easy to establish for school-aged learners, based on the classroom or district curriculum. And parents can extend the theme to the home activities.

Have a 'word(s) of the week'; where the focus is on the word(s) to be learned, rather than the activity or related vocabulary. See how many opportunities for communicating with a single word can be created in multiple activities. Read books that use this word often. Let communication partners outside of the intervention environment know what the word is, so that they, too, can focus on use of this word.

Above all, remember that the efficacy of intervention depends upon the communication partners' belief that the individual can acquire communicative competence.

Teaching to the Individual's Interests:

Motivation is critically important for AAC users to put forth the significant effort needed to learn to use the AAC system. AAC users may tend, without sufficient motivation, to restrict the effort used. The AAC user needs to feel that the goal for this communication instance is worth the effort it will take, and that the goal is attainable and desired.

The attitude of the AAC user and his partners towards the AAC system will also impact his use of it. The user needs to believe that the AAC system will help him become an effective communicator; someone with power. This attitude may be influenced by prior experiences with AAC;

both positive and negative, and by the attitudes of others around him. Overcoming a negative attitude is critical in developing communication.

It has been said that confidence leads to competence. The individual needs to feel the confidence in himself and his AAC system in order to continue to act and interact with it. In an environment where the AAC user does not see others using AAC competently, or interacts with partners who are not themselves competent with using the system, confidence might be difficult to build.

Resilience is what will keep the AAC learner attempting communication with a system that he has yet to learn, with which he experiences some failure. Resilience is the capacity to compensate or overcome problems and to continue trying even after failures. The AAC learner may experience a variety of barriers and lack of success. There may not be acceptance of the AAC system in all of his environments or by all of his partners. The system itself may not be optimal for meeting his needs. Partners that are not trained and/or not familiar with his AAC system can present barriers to using the system.

The communication demands placed on AAC learners also impact development of communicative competence. The social roles of the AAC user influences the types of demands placed upon him. These roles are highly dependent upon the age and situation of the AAC user/learner. Social roles change from infancy through school age, adolescence, young mature and late adulthood. Throughout most of these there is also the role of friendship. Many AAC users find restrictions placed on them by virtue of their AAC use; such as developing the role of friend, significant other, parent, and employee. The communication demands of each of these roles is different, and often difficult.

Interaction goals change within each of these social roles. Light (1988) proposes four main goals of communicative interactions; to express needs and wants, to develop social closeness, to exchange information with others, to fulfill social etiquette expectations.

Light, Beukelman, and Reichle (1988, 2003) list the types of interactions and accompanying communication goals:

Interaction Type	Communication Goal	Communication Demands
Express wants and needs	Regulate behavior of others to get wants and needs met	Get partner's attention, indicate item desired or express rejection, use politeness markers, terminate activity
Develop social closeness	Establish and develop personal relationships	Identify shared topics of interest, make eye contact and attend to partner and provide appropriate feedback, express affect, resolve conflict, continue engagement
Exchange information	To get or give information	Attend to partner's comments or questions, identify opportunities to ask questions or share information, identify new topics, confirm partner's understanding
Fulfill social etiquette	Conform to social conventions of politeness	Identify required opportunities to participate, fulfill these as required, terminate interactions as appropriate

There are a variety of schools of thought about how to begin to provide intervention and where to begin with AAC. Many believe that it is necessary to start at the child's level in order for them to develop functional communication. While there are NO prerequisites to communication, many believe there is a logical order of developmental sequence, with the exception of many practitioners of applied behavior analysis. Too often this leads to underestimation of the learner and restraints on the system provided.

Providing activities that are motivating is the key to learning. If activities are not meaningful and motivating the individual is not engaged. One way to make sure that the activities for learning are motivating is to use the individual's key interests. Often children, in particular, have a key area of interest; such as the current favorite Disney princess, Thomas the Train (or any trains), Legos, sea shells, airplanes, empty boxes.

In general: keep intervention activities fun and novel and student-centered or student-led. Giving students/children the power to control aspects of the situation teaches them the power of communication. Many AAC users have not before had experience with the power of communication. Their environments have been controlled for them. Let them control what activities to engage in, the order in which they do them, and the pace of the activity. Give them vocabulary to express both positive and negative opinions about the activity and ask questions about the activity. Use the student's own interests in meaningful activities. Sometimes, just do something different and unexpected. Attention is enhanced by the novel or unexpected. Remember; motivation is key!

Paula Kluth, in her book, "Just Give Him the Whale," provides a number of anecdotes about how AAC use in students with ASD and Asperger syndrome was significantly increased, by providing users with vocabulary and activities that were based on their key interest. Rather than trying to decrease a student's fascination with a specific topic that consumes much of their interest. She advocates for using it as a tool to engage him in educational activities.

Provide the student with activities that involve the area of interest. Create communication opportunities within these activities and model using appropriate vocabulary within the activity. The focus can be on learning to use a new word for a beginning communicator, but can also apply to learning a syntactic structure or figurative language. Use of motivating themes will engage the individual more and increase learning.

As intervention moves to less contextualized activities, build personal interest story books using PowerPoint/Keynote or similar software, story book creation apps (Pictello, Storybook Maker, Book Creator, Story Patch, Story Creator and others), or TarHeelReader.org. Create books that illustrate vocabulary using illustrations that are relevant to the area of interest. Create stories around the adventures of the character or object using the targeted vocabulary.

Prompting Strategies:

Sometimes individuals require prompts or cues in order to engage in communication; particularly if the skill or vocabulary is new or less motivating. Prompts should be used very carefully and mindfully. Partners should make note of the prompting strategy and level used. Partners should also be very precise in the wording used.

There is a difference between a prompt and a cue. Cues are the stimulus that the partner or environment provides prior to the communication response. It can be environmental, such as a pause in the DVD player that cues the student to make a request. It can be personal, such as the partner asking, "What do you want to drink?"

Move an item into the environment as a cue that it can be talked about. Point to the communication system to cue that there might be something the user should say now.

Provide a verbal cue about what he might say and how. Use an indirect cue to focus the user's attention on an event he might want to talk about. A more direct verbal cue will tell him what to say. Verbal referencing as a cue outlines how to communicate a message. Accomplice suggestion cues are provided when the partner suggests possible messages. A (flash)light cue can be used simply to focus the user's attention. This can be general (just to focus on the AAC system) or specific (focused on the specific target message).

When the individual needs help responding to the cue, a prompt may be used. The prompt may be verbal or gestural. When verbal prompts are used the words must be consistent from partner to partner and be specific. The prompt may be pictorial or written. Picture cues or word cards can be used as a prompt. Gestural prompts are as simple as pointing. Modeling prompts provide a demonstration of what the individual should do. Physical prompts can be light (a touch or tap) or full (hand over hand, also called manual guidance). We never advocate for use of Hand Over Hand in AAC. Remember to use pauses, expectant looks, gestures, repeated models and more expectant pauses. But not manual guidance.

It is always important to allow for a response lag, or wait time, before providing a prompt to the individual. Account for the fact that processing of the initial stimulus may take time. Additional time may be necessary to initiate the motor movement needed to respond. Keep track of the response latency, to see if and how it changes over time or in different situations.

Most often the least-to-most hierarchy of prompts is used (moving from the least prompting - such as gesture - to most intrusive - such as manual guidance – which we should never use in AAC). However, if the individual can follow a gestural cue, prompting should be done with a time delay method, which increases the time between the original stimulus and the gestural prompt. First, most AAC users require extra time to process and begin to compose and make a response. Second, this promotes errorless learning and reduces the user's dependency on prompting. Some students, especially those with autism, can easily become prompt dependent.

According to Erickson, et al (2015), students do not really need continuous prompting and structured practice to learn language (Romski & Sevcik, 2006); but they do need multiple meaningful opportunities to use symbolic language in naturally occurring settings and genuine interactions. They need continuous models of the language system we are asking them to use, embedded into the daily experiences, in a repeated and varied format.

A Word About Partner Training

The AAC user's communication partners are a crucial component of his learning to use his AAC system. Yet, too often, little attention and time are given to training these partners.

"Communication is never just about the individual – and AAC implementation should never be just about the individual either. Speech Language Pathologists are taught to see our interventions as being focused on the client and the individual, but we need to move beyond this. Until we work on and with the whole environment, AAC will not be as successful." (Farrall 2014)

In fact, research suggests that partner training increases AAC users' participation in interactions (Light et al., 1992). Kent-Walsh et al (2015) posit that partner training should be an "integral part" of AAC intervention in every case; particularly as the type of interactions unique to AAC require specific training; per Blackstone (2006) these behaviors are not intuitive.

And why is parent training important? The obvious answer is that the child spends a considerable amount of time in both home and school environments. Parent support has been shown to increase AAC use and competency (Lund & Light, 2007, Gona et al, 2014). Additionally, when parents are not trained, they often see the AAC system as a chore (Lesar, 1998).

But training sessions that involve the clinician talking to the parents alone are not effective (Fixsen, et al, 2005). A more effective model was described by Joyce & Showers, 1980; involving 5 key steps. They suggest describing the strategy, providing models and demonstrations, providing practice, then feedback, and finally coaching that involves observation and feedback over time. In fact, active embedded practice is considered EBP, when it is consistent over time.

There are 3 key skills communication partners need to learn to use:

1. Creating a positive communication environment,

2. Using Partner Augmented Input,

3. And using Sabotage or environmental engineering.

Binger and Kent-Walsh (2012) suggest four guidelines for assisting partners with improving their interaction skills. They have found that trying to change partner behaviors through providing information or suggestions and focusing on too many behaviors at once often fails.

They suggest focusing on the AAC user's skills and the partner's specific behaviors. We should be targeting what the partners are doing that **does** facilitate the learner's AAC use, rather than what is wrong. This helps to avoid defensiveness drowning out anything else you say. Then, target exactly what the partner could do to facilitate better learner outcomes - and what exactly that would look like.

1. Select specific user and partner skills. Focus the instruction on limited skills in limited contexts to experience success and build confidence. Define each skill explicitly, choosing the ones that are easiest to define and change first.

2. Practice the techniques with the AAC user before beginning instruction. This helps to make sure that what you want to teach will work and helps to define what it to be taught. It allows troubleshooting before the fact.

3. Start small, then expand the contexts in which the skill is used. Beginning with a very limited skill in only a very few contexts helps to keep the partner from becoming overwhelmed. Start with an activity that takes less than 15-20 minutes. Stay small. Then you can expand when everyone is experiencing success. Don't try to change too much at once. Once the partner has mastered one context, then expand to another. Continue to select specific and familiar contexts.

Kent-Walsh & McNaughton (2005) listed some behaviors often seen in communication partners that are "less-than-ideal." These include dominating interactions, asking mostly yes/no questions, taking most conversational turns, providing few opportunities for the user to initiate or respond, interrupting, and focusing too much on the technology. Studies show (Douglas 2012) that appropriate training of paraprofessionals resulted in increased skills of AAC users.

So, what constitutes appropriate partner training? Kent-Walsh and Binger (2012) listed 3 approaches that lead not to success, but to frustration; simply talking about the partner's need to change, giving suggestions for how to make these changes, and taking about how it is going. None of these actions actually teach the partner what to do and how to do it. Partners require the skills to change the user's behaviors, and they need to know what the steps are to set them up for success.

Kent-Walsh and McNaughton (2005) proposed "...an 8-step model for communication partner instruction with a strong evidence base..." Kent-Walsh and Binger (2012) developed the ImPAACT Program; Improving Partner Applications of Augmentative Communication Techniques. This program is designed to "..teach communication partners to facilitate the early language and communication skills of children who use AAC." To date, the program has led to improvement across a wide variety of communication forms and functions.

They suggest looking at what kinds of skills are being taught to partners; which should include Aided AAC Modeling, Expectant Delay, Wh-question Asking, and Increased Responsivity. Also, partners need to know when to use these skills. The authors propose several specific techniques to use when targeting partner strategies; including video review (which offers "real world" example, modeling (which provide live demonstrations), role playing (which provides practice with controlled variables), verbal rehearsal (which builds automaticity), and coached practice (which provides constructive feedback).

These strategies do not just tell the partners how to do something, they show how and then provide practice. This involves use of verbal referencing (talking about what you're doing, while you do it).

The stages of their training process are as follows:

Stage 1	Pretest and commit
Stage 2	Strategy description
Stage 3	Strategy demonstration

Stage 4	Verbal practice of strategy steps
Stage 5	Controlled practice with feedback
Stage 6	Advanced practice and feedback
Stage 7	Post-test and commitment to use
Stage 8	Generalization

Ogletree (2012) points out the wide variations in partner education, willingness, degree of commitment, and impact of outside variables, and speaks to the critical involvement of families as resources in intervention. He also speaks of goodness of fit of interventions; so that the interventions also become "feature matched" to the child and their family. He also suggests that the 8 stages of Kent-Walsh and McNaughton's 8 stages be used as a guide, rather than a prescription; that specific stages work best for different family situations.

One group of AAC users who need partner training particularly is those users who cannot use direct selection (point/touch), who either need to learn scanning in order to use switch access to a device, or are learning to use a book or system that requires a partner to assist them for reasons of motor involvement.

One of the key skills for partners of AAC users who need Partner Assisted Scanning is the manner in which they can be "smart partners." Porter has called these communication partners "smart partners" because of the advantages that having a live partner rather than a computerized device scan gives the user.

Electronic devices that are set to scan can only scan at the rate chosen. If the device scans through options either too fast or too slowly, breakdowns occur. The fact that a human scanning can adjust the speed of scanning just by seeing what is going on with the user can be a huge advantage. Partner scanning allows the partner to respond to the subtle - or not so subtle - cues of the user's body language or facial expression, or even vocalizations. Adjusting one's own speech is faster and easier than going into the set-up menu every time the user needs a change in rate due to fatigue, alertness, excitement, boredom, etc.

In Partner Assisted Scanning (PAS) the partner scans through the items by pointing and/or speaking. The partner might show, point, highlight with a light source. The partner might read the labels. Or the partner might do both of those for combined auditory and visual input.

The partner might interpret movements or facial expressions to adjust the rate or, with context cues, interpret the message. While aspects of this skill can be trained, knowledge of the individual user is important.

Partners need to be trained to respond to all communication, to engineer opportunities for expression, and to talk about what they are doing as they model (verbal referencing). Partners need to be trained to give choices first, then list them again slowly; to watch carefully for body cues; and to reduce verbal prompting. Partners need to understand the individual's communication, to understand the individual's movements for communicating, and to know how to use the AAC system.

Partners are responsible for the success of PAS. Using PAS requires practice and consistency. The partner needs to use the vocabulary the individual understands. The partner needs to provide opportunities in the environment, if they are not occurring naturally, for the individual user to use a variety of different responses; including ask/answering, commenting, request/choosing, confirming, soliciting attention/help/escape, etc.

In order to use PAS;

- the partner needs to present the choices one at a time, to allow time between each choice for the individual to

- responds, and to repeat choices for multiple cycles for users who need to hear the choices multiple times before deciding.

- the partner needs to offer choices in a consistent sequence, so that the user with poor reaction time or motor delay can learn to anticipate.

- the partner needs to realize the lack of response doesn't necessarily mean that the user can't choose; there may not be the choice of response the user wants. Systems need to include "something else," or "not what I want," or "different," to indicate this intent.

- the partner needs to learn to decrease the "extra" language that is often mistakenly used to provide additional information or thought to assist the user in making their choice more quickly.

- the partner needs to determine whether the user needs both auditory and visual processing assistance, so they can determine whether to offer visual choices only, auditory choice only, or offer cues in both modes.

- the partner needs to learn to accept all types of responses and to attribute meaning to all responses while providing feedback.

Some specific tips:

Turn-taking is the basis for communication engagement. One person does something, the other person does something to respond or follow. This is how conversations are built. So, how to start building the foundation of turn-taking long before our kids are ready to engage in conversational interactions? Take turns. Start by doing the same thing as the child. Scaffold a response from them, then you repeat the pattern. Say a message and make an action for your turn. Continue to model messages and actions and you go back and forth. Resist the urge to say, "Your turn" and "My turn;" rather make your message match the action. Wait a reasonable time for your child to take a turn, but then prompt or scaffold as necessary to make it happen. If you can, keep the back and forth going for at least 3 turns. If the child isn't actively participating, then stop, but otherwise try to keep it going through modeling and prompting. You can end the interaction by saying, "All done."

Waiting is a good cue all by itself. It helps to decrease the child's dependence on other prompting. Use your body language and facial expressions to indicate you are waiting for the child to do something.

Look "expectant." After a few seconds, point to the activity or item. If necessary, help him to take his turn, but without speaking.

Waiting also serves to foster initiation rather than responding. When we stop filling in all the quiet spaces, we allow time for the child to make a message. And when we stop asking questions, we stop creating interactions where the only thing for him to do is to respond.

Match your child's communication. Do what he does, say what he says. Then you can add just a little bit more. In this way the child sees messages at a level with which he is comfortable, and then at the next level he can try. If your child isn't interacting, for example if he's only banging or throwing a toy, try showing him one thing he can do with that toy. Then add one word or picture to go with it. Adding a message to the action begins to build communication.

Gradually, you can begin to add two word/picture phrases. Don't ask that the child do anything at this point, just continue to match his actions and model simple messages. By putting the focus on actions rather than labels we introduce more meaning into the interaction. A label isn't necessarily communicative. It doesn't indicate what the message is, unless the message is simply, "This is a ___." That is rarely what the child really wants to say.

Try making a comment. This is a model of something he can say, and precludes simply responding to a question.

Remember, too, to carefully attach meaning to what you are saying to the child. Make the words you use have a meaning that is clear to the child and to the context. Many of the teachers and parents I know want to teach the child to say "Please" and "Thank you" and often use terms like "Good job" or "Good boy" or even "That's good." These words don't have meaning attached to them, and may even cause the child to attach the wrong meaning. Be specific about the words you use and make sure they are meaningful.

Engineering the environment provides multiple opportunities for communicating that might not ordinarily arise. Changing the environment to change the need to communicate increases the opportunities for the child to learn to use his messages. One of the easiest ways to do this is to make it more difficult for the child to access the desired items and activities. Be careful not to do this so much that you frustrate him. Do it just enough to provide increased opportunities for him to need to communicate to get what he wants.

One part of engineering the environment can be to create scripts to use in an activity beforehand. Think about the activity and the items and actions involved. Make sure you know where the words are located in the AAC system. Create an activity-based page if it is appropriate and is a repeating activity. For example, I play a lot with bubbles as that is often a preferred activity for kids with whom I work. So, on my toys page, where I have my bubbles button, the bubbles button links to a bubbles activity page. There I have the pronouns involved (you, I, it), the actions (blow, catch, pop, wipe), more and again and all done. I also have descriptive words like high and low, big and little to direct and describe. Now you have a plan and the tools needed for interacting in a given activity.

In addition, the most important thing we can do for our AAC users is to be the model communication partner. Using an AAC system to communicate TO the child AAC effectively, of how to find needed vocabulary in the AAC system, and of what kinds of word to use for what purposes. I've spoken before about Aided Language Stimulation - also called Partner Aided Input. But I think it cannot be said enough.

What else can you do? Try parallel talk and self-talk. Describe what is going on right now. What are you doing? What do you think about it? What is the child doing? Comment on it. Break down the messages. Provide a message and then repeat the key words only. This is called breaking down the message. Building up the message is done by providing key words, then repeating the message with more elements to clarify the meaning. For example, "Snack time. It's time to have a snack." Provide input at the child's level, but also at a step above. And remember, provide this input verbally, but also on the AAC system.

Also try looking carefully at what the child is doing. Often communication attempts are missed because we are not paying careful attention to what the child is doing. Be sure to respond to those attempts, and, if necessary, ascribe meaning to them. Above all else, keep communication fun and functional!

What should you not do? Don't dominate the interactions. Don't ask yes/no questions most of the time. Don't take the majority of conversational terms. Don't interrupt the AAC user. Don't restrict the opportunities for the AAC user to interact, respond, initiate. Don't focus on the technology instead of the person using it. (Kent-Walsh & McNaughton 2005).

Sabotage: The strategy of presenting situations that the child needs to solve in order to get what he wants. This creates a barrier in the environment that the child needs to overcome. It was originally developed by Goossens et al (1992) to promote AAC use. I like Musselwhite's phrase, "creatively managing the environment." She categorizes types of sabotage; incorrect item, missing item, omitted step, incomplete step

Temptations: Basically, just a nicer-sounding way of creating the same situations. We set up the environment to reveal something that the child wants - that tempts him - so he will communicate that to us.

For example, I might set up a race track but not give the child a car until he asks. I might give him an empty cup or plate and wait for him to ask for the snack or drink. I might give all the other children in the group a cookie, except for him.

Setting up situations that tempt can be easy; there are many opportunities throughout the day. Weatherby & Prizant (1989) formalized the term "communication temptations;" specifying that there needs to be "… a need, an opportunity, and a reward for his…efforts." Some of the examples in their book:

- Offer your child something to eat you know he doesn't like.

- Put a toy in a container that he can't see through. Shake it until he shows interest.

- Wave good-bye and say "bye" while putting toys into a container 3 times. Then pause before you put the next one in.

- Sit down and read a book he likes, but hold it up-side-down or backwards.

- Activate a wind-up toy and let it run down. Hand it to the child.

As with many strategies, you need to make sure that your child experiences success, not frustration!

When I do evaluations, one of the most popular activities I have is watching a DVD. I have a wide range of movies available and I let the child choose. A few minutes into the movie I hit "Pause," and wait while looking at the child expectantly. I can also say, "Uh oh!" If needed, I can model, "more," or "go," and turn it back on.

I repeat this process, being careful not to make the child frustrated. I can extend the time between pauses to keep him engaged, but not enough to saturate him or make him say, "All done."

I can often go from "more," to "more movie," to "want more," and "want more movie" within a single session, with the child imitating my model throughout.

Some other examples:

Activity:	Possibility for temptation/sabotage
washing hands	remove towel, put soap on hands but don't turn on the water
play with trains	run train off table, hold onto train instead of pushing it back to him
eat breakfast	forget utensils, give the wrong utensil, put favorite item out of reach

Jennifer Kent-Walsh & David Mcnaughton (2005) Communication Partner Instruction in AAC: Present Practices and Future Directions,

Augmentative and Alternative Communication, 21:3, 195-204, DOI: 10.1080/07434610400006646

CHAPTER 6

200 opportunities a day - how?

C hildren need a minimum of 200 opportunities each day to become proficient AAC users. They need to learn multiple communication functions. And they need to see others using pictures to communicate effectively.

Opportunities to use aided language input and elicit AAC use occur all throughout the day. Research has shown that it takes 200 opportunities per day for an AAC user to learn to use their system effectively. * (See Appendix)

Partners often think that this is a huge number that cannot possibly be achieved. However, they are usually surprised at how easily 200 opportunities add up. Baker et al (2011) suggest a number of ways and times to build communication:

> Morning Activities: opportunities around taking roll call and initial greetings as well as calendar time activities

> Cooking and Snack: opportunities beyond requesting include commenting about the food, sequencing steps of a cooking activity, and verbalizing whose turn it is.

> Literacy: add repetitive lines and generic book reading responses into systems

Leisure: play is not a "free for all," but opportunities to provide structure of communication responses. Commenting, taking turns, and verbs associated with the activities.

Often the most important target skill for our students is gaining attention appropriately. Take a look at gestures or behaviors that they already exhibit. Then think about how you can shape or modify that feature or behavior into something more appropriate or universally understood.

One strategy that I have mentioned before that can be used to create opportunities has been alternately called creating communication temptations, sabotage, or engineering the environment. This involves arranging - or rearranging - the environment so that there is a need or desire to communicate in order get at what the child wants; whether that is an object, person, activity, or feeling.

This is easily arranged to promote requesting by putting the item out of reach, or only providing a limited amount of it, or managing the environment in some other way so that the AAC user needs to make a request.

Comments can be engineered through the use of deliberate miscalculation or error. Opening a favorite book up-side-down to read it, crashing the trains or cars on the play mat, rolling the ball in the wrong direction, putting a puzzle piece in the wrong place or orientation are all examples of ways to misguide the situation, providing opportunities to comment "Oh, no!" or "Not that," or "Help."

Within the context of every interaction is at least one, if not multiple, opportunity(ies). During any play interaction the partner can model a comment (it fun, this is fun, like, I like this, look, look at that, etc.) ... The partner then waits with the expectant signal and, if needed, prompts a response. Continued modeling, waiting, and prompting forms a continuous loop of communicating and creating communication opportunities.

During a snack or other eating time, partners can create the need to model requests, demonstrating, or directing with words such as; "that" "that one" "want that" "give that" "want more" "I want some" "open it" "help please" etc. Model, wait expectantly, prompt.

Once again, inserting that wait time is crucial. Too often communication partners do not wait long enough for the individual to respond.

Other examples of creating opportunities within the environment include:

Making a favorite item inaccessible - don't automatically offer the item when the child reaches or cries or tugs at you.

Provide an example of "Help" or "Want" or "Give" or "Get." Be careful with this strategy, so as to avoid frustration.

Giving small portions - be careful with this strategy, too, to avoid frustration. Cut an apple into pieces and don't provide the whole apple at once. On the other hand, don't provide only 1/8 of the apple at a time, hoping to maximize communication opportunities. Model "Give" or "More"

Creating a need for assistance - place a desired item into a sealed container, or out of reach, move the remote control for the T.V. or DVD player. Provide models for "Help" and "Want" and "Go."

Interrupting a favorite activity - blow bubbles only 1 or 2 times and wait, watch a part of a show then pause it, provide 2 colors of crayons but not the rest. Provide models for "More" and "Go" and "Do."

Offering something the individual does not like - model "No" or "Not" or "Different" or "Stop"

Providing an activity with a part missing - model "Want" or "Give" or "Help" or "More."

Offer surprises - these can be good or "bad" surprises. Usually, the unexpected mess provokes a reaction; such as dropping the bowl of popcorn or box of puzzle pieces. Model "Oh no" or "Yuck." Good surprises can also provoke a reaction of course. Bring out a favorite item, snack, or activity. Model 'Yay" or "Mine" or "Good"

Select a book you know the child doesn't like. Model, "No," "Yuck," "Different."

Start reading in the middle of the book. Model "Go back," "Start over," "Turn page."

Stop reading too soon. Model, "More," Turn page," "Go."

Hold the book up-side-down. Model, 'Wrong," "Turn," "Do different."

Start at the back of the book. Model, "Wrong," "Go back," "Turn back."

Overall, it is important not to anticipate the child's needs all the time; instead create more needs to communicate. Engineering the environment has been used for decades to teach communication skills in both speaking and nonspeaking individuals. It creates opportunities for communication in the natural environment; teaching skills in context. It also eliminates a need for generalization from the intervention environment to the natural environment.

Model, "I need help," "Get it," "Want it," "Mine," "You do." Teaching individuals to use AAC is an on-going process that needs to be participated in by all of the individual's communication partners. There need to be systematic strategies provided to AAC learners for organizing and using the vocabulary in the AAC system, and easy access to the wide variety of vocabulary needed to communicate effectively. There are several strategies that are common to teaching almost all AAC learners.

The assessment process needs to be thought of as on-going, not just done once and set. Even where the individual is assessed in an isolated assessment center, the communication partners that continue to support him need to be constantly monitoring the process, the progress, and the barriers; making adjustments to the system or the intervention as needed. This constant monitoring almost never ends. Both the individual and the technology change over time, often very quickly. This may not impact all users, but can significantly impact others.

One of the problems with high-technology dedicated systems is the ever-changing profile of the computer and AAC industries. Sometimes, by the time an individual's system requires repairs the device is no longer manufactured - or even supported - and a new device needs to be purchased, requiring a new evaluation report if funding is being sought through medical insurance. This problem is also seen with using the iPad and an AAC app; the app market fluctuates widely, needs constant revision with the roll-out of each new iOS, and app developers abandon apps as their returns dwindle.

Implementation of AAC can be challenging. This may be due to lack of acceptance or buy-in by teaching and support staff or by the AAC user. It may be due to the system not meeting the user's needs. Or it may simply be due to lack of training. A structured implementation plan is extremely helpful in keeping everyone on track and giving users and partners a roadmap to follow. Important to include are frequent structured opportunities, instructions for taking very small steps one at a time, training information and opportunities for partners.

How well an individual develops competency with his AAC system is strongly influenced by the competencies of his partners, their degree of supportiveness, and any barriers they place in his way. Communication partners can either be a source of support or an impediment. The policies of the school environment, workplace, or living space can also be either supportive or hindering.

One example of a barrier faced is when school districts limit the use of the AAC system to the classroom, or to the building itself; prohibiting the student from take the AAC system home with him for practice there.

Barriers may also exist when there are limited trained professionals available to provide services, or when insurance companies put limits on the amount of intervention services they will pay for.

Attitude barriers impede the progress of the AAC user when partners have low expectations of the user, when partners do not accept the AAC system, or when it is not believed that the AAC user can compete in natural contexts with others. Attitude support may be needed to provide more of a positive "can-do" message that fosters development in the AAC user.

Knowledge barriers occur when there is not sufficient quality information available about AAC. Partners may not be appropriately trained. Professionals themselves may not have sufficient knowledge and training.

Skill barriers exist when AAC is not implemented effectively. This is one of the greatest causes of "abandonment" of AAC. When appropriate AAC intervention strategies are not applied the individual may become frustrated. Partners may not see progress. When partners fail to respond to communication attempts the entire system can break down.

How to combat some of the barriers? Make therapy curriculum driven. Balance the student's need to learn language while simultaneously using that language to learn in the classroom, while also learning how to operate the AAC system.

Give the student the power to control the session to some extent. Allow the student to choose what activities to do, what order to do them in, the pace of the activity and give him the opportunity - and tools - to express opinions both positive and negative. All too often intervention is clinician- (or adult-) led, and students have minimal opportunity to even respond, let alone initiate or lead.

Show the child the choice of activities and let them choose what to do first, next, last. Give them some power over the length of the activity or how many items to complete before they can say, "Want different."

I spoke earlier about using activities that are meaningful to the student. Having activities that revolve around his interests will maximize motivation. Does your student love trains? Put picture symbols on train cards and have the student line them up into sentences. Use train pictures to show how many tasks need to be completed. Put rhyming words on train cards and have them go by pairs into the 'train station.' Use characters from the theme's series to illustrate concepts. Read a Thomas or other train story; then have the student sequence the events in the story, describe each train, etc.

Use favorite characters. How many things can Sponge Bob do? He is running. He is jumping. Sponge Bob is going to the market. What will he find in the produce section? Where will he find ice cream? What does he like to do? Can you tell how he feels about this? Why does he look happy?

Use what is happening in the environment. Both in class and at home, there are usually other people. Ask the AAC user to identify "Who is sitting?" "He is." "Who is yelling?" "She is." Build verbs simply by using what is going on around you. Remember what I said about verbal referencing? Now is a good time to provide "Who questions are answered by people words. Where are the people in your AAC system? Where are the pronouns?"

Students can practice to learn the construct in therapy, then generalize on the playground, in class, at home. Simply choose the target skill and look in the environment for examples. And, if need be, create those examples in the environment.

Remember always that our goal is not about labeling more things, or making more requests, but about increasing the number of communication functions the child can use; including regulating what others do, discussing, describing, commenting, questioning. Being able to produce messages for a variety of intents - even with the simplest constructs - is a major accomplishment. And it is much more functional than being able to label 10 - or even 100 - more things.

To model commenting, for example, consider these turns:

"There is (object, color, person). What do you see?"

"I like (food, color, place, toy, show). What do you like?"

"I have (show or name item). What do you have?"

"I really like (activity, show, object). What do you think?"

"I'm finished with (activity). What about you?"

Try the old therapy standard; start with a paper bag or pile of assorted items. The communication partner models telling about 1 item. Then ask child to tell about one. You can say, "It is (red, bumpy, little, sticky…). I (like it, don't like, think it's yucky…)"

Give a choice of 2-3 items (objects or pictures) and the cue, "Tell me about one of these." Practice using the carrier phrase, "It is…+ adjective." In a group or one on one, the communication partner picks an item and says, "It is (adjective). You tell me about one." Use a time delay prompting strategy to reduce prompt dependency (time delay is explained in the appendix). The communication partner (CP) would first provide an immediate model, then add a delay of (X) seconds before giving a model; increasing the delay as the student progresses.

Riddles - I live in a bowl, I can swim, I have a tail, I have fins and big eyes, I am a ____ (find me on your AAC system); I am the fifth planet from the sun, 4th brightest object in the sky, I am named for the king of gods. What am I? (You might not find me in your AAC system, but you can probably find me on a curriculum topic board.

Now try it the other way around. Teach users to provide referential definitions. I am (category), I am (describing words), I am found in (place), I (action, function, materials).

Arts & Crafts: Plan out your core words - think about the sequence of actions in the process.

I opened

I painted

I like __

You paint it

Can you open it?

Do more

Different color?

All done

Stop

Snack: Plan out your core words - think about the sequence of actions in the process.

I like	Help open
He likes	All done
You like	Don't like
Not me	Want more?
Need help?	Look

Cooking: Plan out your core words - think about the sequence of actions in the process.

Pour in	Bake	It is hot	Roll	Do you like?
Stir it	Eat it	I like	Too hot	

Watch a movie: Plan out your core words - think about the sequence of actions in the process.

Go	Not that	Turn on	This one	I like
Don't like	Want more	Want different	Too loud	

Bubbles: Plan out your core words - think about the sequence of actions in the process.

Blow	Blow more	All done
Up high	More	Uh oh! Spilled Do again
Look there	You do Pop	Catch

Nail Polish: Plan out your core words - think about the sequence of actions in the process.

That one	Put it on	Take it off
Different	Like	I don't like
Oops	It pretty	Do more
Mess	Fix it	

More with single core words:

1. Print or copy single important core words. Use them to request (I want, want that, give, get), to greet (Hi, hello, hey there, bye), accept or reject (yes, no, don't, not), to protest (stop, away, don't, not), to direct (there, here, give, get, put), to continue or cease (different, go, stop, more), indicate possession (my, mine, your, his), to participate (repeated line, specific response).

2. Go on a vocabulary scavenger hunt. Using books and magazines with pictures and text highlight specific vocabulary. Talk about the vocabulary. Have student/child find the vocabulary in his AAC system.

3. Look around the room again. What color markers are on the table? How many are there? What do you do with markers? Where are "markers" in your AAC system? Practice possessives: "Whose hat is that?" Practice pronouns; "Who is [doing X]? He is."

    And remember, while working on morphology and syntax is important, for early communicators the emphasis is on the message, not the grammar.

4. Put words/pictures/symbols on cards in a bag. Participants take turns pulling a random card out of the bag. They need to find the item in their AAC system, or describe the item using their AAC system, or answer questions about the item using their AAC system. This can also be played with common items and students need to tell the item function using their AAC system.

5. Take photos of the student/child and peers or family members in various activities. Create a word bank of pronouns and verbs; then have the student construct a phrase or sentence using the symbol/word bank. Once (s)he can do this, move into the AAC system and navigate to each symbol needed.

6. Make an assortment of symbol cards for Go-Fish or Memory-type games. Practice finding words in the AAC system while also practicing turn-taking and game commenting. Try an antonym Go Fish or opposites Memory game.

   Sort by adjective, initial sound, same or different. Do you see why we need that robust vocabulary? It does not need to be comprehensive in the beginning. For riddles, all you need is a page with more than 2 animals, plants, foods or other category.

7. Another game that can be used with core words, curricular content words, or a variety of basic concept words involves making cards with 3-4 members of a category. Students pick a card and find that category in their AAC systems.

8. Pick an image of a piece of clothing, make multiple copies, each with a different texture on it (rough, sticky, smooth, etc.) ... Hang the clothing cards on a "clothesline." (This can be a real string with clothespins or a page with a clothesline (just a curved line). Students pick pictures of different items with specific recognizable textures. They match the item on their card with a texture on the clothesline. If you have students who find it difficult to pick the cards up, glue them to actual clothespins.

9. Make BINGO cards with thematic vocabulary. Instead of calling out the word, call out a description or definition. Students have to figure out what the item is before they can mark it on their card.

10. Try a thematic "Guess Who" game. The popular Milton-Bradley game is a favorite with SLPs for good reason. Pat Mervine has suggested a thematic version using other creatures; "Does your creature have…?" Try claws, wings, tail, fur, feathers, etc.

11. Time to clean up? Turn it into a preposition activity. Put the book inside the desk. Put the markers in the jar. Put the paper on top of the table. Put the chair next to the desk. "You tell me..." turns the power over to the student who now needs to use his AAC system to give you directions. For young students, use a stuffed animal or action/play figure and have them put it in between, inside, on top, next to, etc.

12. Categorize items from the general education curriculum. Sort acids v. bases, carnivores v. omnivores, spicy v. sweet, predators v. prey.

13. Create core word cards and see how many phrases and sentences the individual can make out of them. This will increase as you continue to add core words. As descriptive words are added, they can be used to elaborate on a concept.

14. Create core word books. Have the child find pictures and words to put in the books. It is easy to create books around descriptive vocabulary; such as colors and sizes, and spatial location concepts; such as in, on, under, and next to. Other concepts are easy to represent in books; such as things the child likes, or things that make the student happy or sad.

15. Create stories around each new word, in conjunction with previously learned words. Have the individual raise a hand, make a vocalization, or use some other signal when he hears you use the word. Use the word in different sentences and have the AAC user determine if it was used correctly or incorrectly.

16. Create books that revolve around specific concept vocabulary. Include pictures and even easy-to-glue-in objects or fragments. Find pictures in magazines and books. Have the individual determine whether a picture represents a word, or its opposite.

17. Have a single message button - like a Big Mack - to use? Some messages for these: help, more, stop, go, all done, don't, make, play, eat, drink, read, sleep.

18. Have a talking photo album? Make a shopping list, picture recipes, retell an event, give personal information, list the steps of an activity; make flash cards, make a picture menu, make a book report, take attendance, sing a song, create social stories, tell someone about your family or friends.

19. Have a sequencer button? Program lines from a simple story. Tell a joke. Go back to those steps of an activity, shopping list, or book report. Have a randomizer button? Play Simon Says, be the BINGO caller, cheer on a sports team.

Among the important functions to teach your AAC users:

- Gaining attention - one of the most important skills for our students. Does the individual already have gestures or actions or vocalizations to signal desire for attention? Are these not always appropriate or universally understood? Can you shape them into something more acceptable and recognized?

- Commenting - during an activity or story, model comments such as; Cool, Awesome, Terrible, Bad, Wow! Model, then create a dramatic expectant pause.

- Conversation - provide sufficient social vocabulary. Build peer interactions outside of academics. provide vocabulary to ask questions, make comments and interjections. Have the student choose a topic that is interesting/exciting/important to him. Work with him to generate some things to say to start the conversation, tell what he wants to say, add a comment and/or question, and close the conversation. Then program the sequence into his AAC device. (Musselwhite & Burkhart, 19) "Can We Chat?" and "Anatomy of a Social Script" @ http://www.aacintervention.com

- If your user doesn't have a robust AAC system yet, make conversation rings; a series of symbols on small cards put together on a binder ring. Or make a conversation notebook for selected topics.

Ultimately, we all need fringe words. Fringe vocabulary are those words that are more situation or individual specific. Their importance changes from context to context and from person to person (e.g., evaporation, condense, pyramid). We use fringe words about 20% of the time. Students usually use fringe words more in classroom content situations. Fringe vocabulary that is individual-specific often needs to be added to AAC systems, and needs to be done without disturbing the stability of the core words. With communication books this usually means adding pages of fringe words above, behind, or to the side of the core word board. In high-tech devices these are the pages to which users may need to navigate in order to have a more robust and specific vocabulary.

Communicating is about more than the vocabulary; it's about being able to have shared experiences and to share experiences. Teaching AAC users how to construct narratives, and/or what basic information or word types need to be included is very important, particularly when we want them to 1) move beyond requesting and 2) be able to tell about the day. Developing narratives allows people to tell about recent events and activities, and to tell and re-tell stories.

Working on narrative production is something we do with neuro-typical kids in classrooms every day, but rarely do with our AAC users. Too often they don't have either sufficient vocabulary or syntax.

So, how can you promote this ability? According to a study by Soto et al (2013) we can use personal photographs of a recent experience or event that is emotionally charged. It can be something that evokes a happy feeling, or a sad one; an experience that made the student laugh or smile or even cry (if it will not make the child feel upset).

Ask the child if he recalls the event. Use open-ended questions, a story map, and elicitation strategies to ask the student to tell you about and describe the event. Write down everything the AAC user "says," and when he is done you can "decorate" what he has said in order to expand the language and provide a model of better form. Make sure to cover all the basic Whs.

When vocabulary is not available, model the use of circumlocution; use the beginning sound, use a sign, provide the category/function/location, say, "It rhymes with…" When complete, the communication partner (you) programs the story into the device or create a story board for later use.

For example, I worked with a teenager who has severe cerebral palsy, spastic type. She came in with a picture of a trip to the Wild Animal Park. Through use of Partner Assisted Scanning with her PODD book, she was able to say:

1. I'm telling you something -> it already happened
2. Category -> places -> Wild Animal Park
3. Category -> people -> Mom, Dad, Jennifer
4. Category -> animals -> bird, giraffe
5. Category -> special occasion -> vacation
6. Opinion -> I like it

Note that the emphasis is on the comments and the message; not on syntax. This will come later. We do need to teach syntax and morphology and grammar. But we can start with narrative formulation even at the one-word utterance stage.

From there, I helped her construct the following:

1. I want to tell you something that happened
2. I went to the Wild Animal Park
3. I went with Mom, Dad, and Jennifer

4. I saw birds and giraffes

5. I went over vacation

6. I liked it.

She then had me re-order the sentences into her story:

"I want to tell you about something. I went to the Wild Animal Park. I went over vacation. I went with Mom, Dad, and Jennifer. I saw birds and giraffes. I liked it."

Then her aide modeled use of expanded sentences and correct syntax. From there they developed the following improved narrative:

"I want to tell you what I did over vacation. Mom, Dad, Jennifer and I went to the Wild Animal Park. I saw birds and giraffes. I really liked it."

The narrative was programed into her high-tech device on a "stories" page that has the main photo in the center of the page with 4 buttons on the side, where it is easier for her to reach.

Story narratives are also used to develop language skills, because of structural similarities between personal narratives and story re-telling. Topic maintenance, event sequencing, use of elaboration and referencing, and a need for fluency are all important in academic and social situations.

Narratives are the base of conversations. In a conversation we are usually telling someone about something. We need sufficient vocabulary for social situations, in order for the AAC user to build peer interactions outside of academics, and for students to ask questions, respond, make comments, and make interjections.

Remember that sequencer button when we were talking about low tech message buttons? Have the child choose a topic. Work with him to generate some things to say to start the conversation, tell what he wants to say, add a comment, and close the conversation. Program these on the sequencer button.

"Guess what I did last night.

I went to the basketball game.

It was cool to see our team.

Maybe we can go together some time.

See ya later."

For more conversation building, check out Musselwhite and Burkhart's "Can We Chat?" program and "Anatomy of a Social Script" at http://www.aacintervention.com.

Would it be better if he had a more comprehensive SGD? Sure. It's just not always immediately possible, and the sequencer is a great addition to a robust AAC system.

Other no-tech or light-tech conversation options?

1. Sets of conversational rings - pictures of selected topics held on binder rings

2. Pages of pictures for selected topics in a notebook

3. How-to pages for a PODD user partner with a list of page turns needed for selected topics for practice

AAC users don't need different activities; they need practice.

More Decontextualized Activities

Eventually, adding decontextualized activities serves a couple of purposes. First, it builds the speed and ease with which the AAC user can locate vocabulary in the AAC system. Working on fluency outside of communication contexts relieves the user of the pressure to find the word while a partner is waiting. Also, decontextualized practice provides additional generalization of and practice with using the word. Practice and more practice is the answer to using vocabulary in the AAC system.

iOS apps are being used increasingly in intervention. Many apps designed for children's entertainment provide excellent opportunities for generating language. The Toca Boca apps are often used by SLPs to generate language in therapy sessions. They can be used equally well to practice core word use and phrase or sentence use.

For example, Toca Tea Party provides multiple opportunities to make requests (want that, want tea, want this one, not that one, want cake, want more, want different one, want punch), to comment (like that, don't like, you eat, I eat it, uh oh, all done, need more, it spill), to direct (give me that one, put it there, put, give, have, move, wipe, eat, drink, take a bite, wash them), to describe (pink one, green, flowers, red and white, pretty, little, messy, dirty to question (want more? want this? which one? you finish? play again?)

Bamba Burger provides players with a burger restaurant where one can make a custom burger. Choose the bun, cook the burger, and choose the toppings. All of these options provide lots of opportunity to make requests, make comments (sardines on your burger? "Yuck."), give directions and descriptions, ask questions, and more. Players also choose style of fries, flavor of soda, amount to pay.

Play Home is a virtual doll house complete with a family of virtual dolls and rooms full of furniture. Just like any doll house is used in intervention to elicit language, the app can be used to give AAC learners the opportunity to give directions, describe locations, ask questions, and more.

Above all, talk about what you are doing throughout activities. Providing good language input throughout activities, talking about words as you are teaching them, talking about why a word is used here, but not there, or can look like this but not that - all of this is what builds language skills.

Story books, as I've suggested before, are excellent sources for intervention. You can use stories to increase vocabulary, story grammar, narrative skills, and syntax. And using books continues to build on narrative structure for telling personal stories as well as fiction.

Narrative teaching strategies are just as useful for teaching picture- or text-based language strategies as they are for oral students (or even more so) Because students get engaged with the problems and actions in a show, characters and setting become the natural medium for learning language.

Narrative teaching strategies include (but are not limited to); compare/contrast diagrams, thinking activities, episode and story maps, journals, semantic word maps, story retellings, summarizing, story generating, and internal states charts.

These are the same strategies good SLPs, teachers, and even some parents are already using. What usually prevents students/children from participating in these activities is lack of access to sufficient vocabulary.

Shared reading is, "[t]he interaction that occurs when a child and adult look at or read a book together. (Ezell & Justice, 2005). Students who cannot yet read, who may or may not be interested in books, who have not yet developed a symbolic mode of communication, and even those who can read but still need continual support to get meaning from text all benefit from shared reading times.

During shared reading times the focus is on interacting with the story and gaining meaning from it. Adults read with the students rather than to them, and gradually transition the reading from themselves to the children. These shared reading opportunities build receptive and expressive language skills at the same time as they build emergent literacy and communication skills.

Communication Levels and AAC Interventions

Light (1989) has delineated four areas of competence that need to be developed in AAC users:

Linguistic Competency

In addition to learning the general receptive and expressive language skills typically developed by all individuals, AAC users need also to learn the linguistic code of the particular AAC system and symbol system that they are learning to use. They need to learn the meaning of the symbols, and how to use them and combine them to construct desired messages. Because the AAC system may use symbols, words, or letters, it is different from the linguistic system of expressive language used by others in the individual's environment. This is further confounded by the lack of phonological, semantic, syntactic features of the AAC system's language.

Operational Competency

Operational skills are those needed to learn how to operate the system and access the symbols it uses. They include the skills needed to form hand shapes of signs, sequence the motor movements needed to find, reach, and activate the symbol buttons. Operational skills are necessary to not only operate the individual components of the system, but to learn to do so in a way that minimizes both the impact of fatigue and the time it takes to produce a message. Operational skills are impacted by the cognitive, motor, linguistic, and sensory perceptual capabilities of the user.

Social Competency

Social skills are those that allow the individual to utilize those linguistic and operational skills to effect competency in communication with others. Light proposed that there are 2 types of social skills required for communication: sociolinguistic and sociorelational skills.

Sociolinguistic skills are typically referred to as pragmatic skills. These skills include the strategies needed for discourse; such as, turn taking, topic initiation and maintenance, communicative functions.

Sociorelational skills are those that involve judgement, knowledge, and skills in interpersonal relationships. These may include being responsive to a partner, actively participating in the exchange, taking interest in the communication partner, engaging in interactions, maintaining rapport with partners, putting partners at ease.

Strategic Competency

AAC users' development of linguistic, operational and social competencies are all impacted by the limitations of their various disorders, and by the limitations of the AAC system itself. Despite intervention, AAC users may be restricted by the limits of what the AAC system can provide for them. A child who is not literate yet, for example, is dependent upon others to provide vocabulary for him to use and may often find situations in which he does not have the word that he needs for the context. A severely involved individual with cerebral palsy may be reliant on switch scanning access to the AAC system, and therefore not be able to maintain the speed of interaction in typical conversational exchanges.

In these and other instances the AAC user will need to develop strategies to optimize efficient and effective communication with the limits of the system itself. Strategic competence can allow the AAC user to attain communicative competence in spite of the linguistic, operational, or social impairments.

Case example: Martin was an 18-year-old young man with severe cerebral palsy, spastic quadriplegia. Martin's parents had become frustrated with the school district's lack of effective education for their son. Tired of teachers who either thought he wasn't capable of learning or didn't know how to teach him, they took Martin out of school at age 16. He was sent to an Adult Day Program with other persons with cerebral palsy. At this program Martin was lucky to find staff who knew something about AAC and had the materials to provide him with a beginning system. They created a categorical or topical picture communication book with multiple pages. They taught Martin about Partner Assisted Scanning. Within a short amount of time, they were able to hold up a page, ask him if what he wanted to say was on that page and move through the pages quickly until he indicated the one he wanted. They then scanned across the rows of pictures on that page until he got to the row that held the pictured message he wanted. They then scanned across the row to find what Martin wanted to say.

When an AAC assessment was available in their area, Martin's parents brought him to the Assistive Technology Center for an assessment. A staff of two speech-language pathologists and a physical therapist found a system that would work for him, including a high-tech dynamic display device and a switch for scanning access. A wheelchair mount was ordered so that the device was always on his wheelchair.

When the system arrived at the center, Martin and his family came to pick it up. Once it was mounted on his wheelchair and the switch scanning access set up, Martin used a combination of symbols with words and the keyboard to type out the message, "Thank you so much for giving me a voice. Now I can speak like everyone else."

No one had ever taught Martin literacy skills. He had sat in the back of the classroom for 10 years.

Martin is, of course, an exception and a truly exceptional young man. Most students require specific direct instruction, multiple opportunities with good support, and - of course - an effective AAC system.

Structured opportunities for communication should include the discriminative stimulus; what you say or do to elicit a response. In the Model - Expectant Pause - Prompt - Respond model of input, that Model and/or the Expectant Pause are what the partner does to elicit a response. The response is then what the AAC user says or does, with or without a prompt. The consequence is the feedback the communication partner gives. This can be a continuation of the interaction, a repetition with or without recasting what the AAC user has said, a reinforcing phrase for what was said.

These opportunities should be integrated into the everyday activities and interactions of the individual. They should be provided by everyone who works with the student, as well as at home by all caregivers and other communication partners.

Rowland and Schweigert, (1997) created a construct of 7 levels of communicative abilities that help in assessments (See Rowland's Communication Matrix) and intervention:

Level 1. Unintentional behavior: Behavior is not under the individual's control, but reflects his general state (comfortable, hungry, etc.). Caregivers interpret the individual's state from behaviors such as body movements, facial expressions, and sounds. In typically developing children this stage occurs between 0 and 3 months.

Level 2. Intentional behavior: Behavior is under the individual's control, but not yet used to communicate intentionally. Individuals at this stage don't yet realize they can use behaviors to control another person's behavior. Caregivers continue to interpret the individual's needs based on the behaviors. This usually is between 3 and 8 months of age.

Level 3. Unconventional communication (pre-symbolic): This is where intentional communication begins. Unconventional pre-symbolic behaviors are used intentionally to communicate. Communicative behaviors do not yet involve any sort of symbol, nor are they socially acceptable for use as the individual ages. Communicative behaviors include body movements, facial expressions, vocalizations, and simply gestures such as tugging on someone. It typically occurs between 6 and 12 months of age.

Typical children move through the pre-symbolic on their way to more complex communication. Pre-symbolic communication can be effective, but for a limited range of function and only in the here and now. Moving to symbolic communication is the only way to communicate about things/events/etc. beyond the immediate environment and context.

Many individuals with severe disabilities of all ages use a variety of behaviors to express themselves; not all of which are deemed appropriate or acceptable by others in their culture. Some of these can be destructive to themselves or their environment. Individuals may pull out their hair or bite themselves when angry or frustrated. They may hit the wall or others when upset or to get attention. They might throw objects or break them. These behaviors may continue to be used because they have had some function reinforced. They might gain the user access to a desired item, or escape from an unpleasant or difficult task, or attention from someone.

Moving these unconventional communicative behaviors to more conventional and symbolic communication involves a replacement behavior that is equally communicative, equally easy to do, and gains an equal response needs to be discovered and then used consistently by the communication partners. A careful functional analysis of the behaviors will determine their function or the communicative intent, so that intervention can be effective. In MOVE UP Carol Goosens delineated 4 guidelines for Aided Language Stimulation:

Use primarily single words/symbols and short but grammatically correct phrases to talk about what the child does, sees, hears, and feels.

Use lots of repetition as you describe ongoing events.

Speak slowly, inserting numerous pauses into the conversational flow

Whenever the child indicates something with a single word/symbol, expand that message into a semantically equivalent two word/symbol combination

Level 4. Conventional communication (pre-symbolic): Communication behaviors do not yet use symbols but are socially acceptable and individuals continue to use them as they age or mature. They include pointing, nodding, shaking the head, waving, hugging, and looking from the partner to a desired item. These may involve vision skills, so are not appropriate for all individuals with vision impairments. There may also be some vocalizations used. This stage is usually from 12-18 months.

Typical children at 12-18 months may already be using symbolic communication. They usually have 20-100 words and use a variety of communication behaviors. Examples, provided by The NC Department of Public Intervention, include existence (ball, mama, juice), nonexistence (no more, all gone, no), recurrence (more), rejection (no), denial (no), attribution (big, dirty, broken), possession (mine, mommy), action (wash, play, eat, drink), locative action (go, sit, up, out, there).

Level 5. Concrete symbols. This is the beginning of symbolic communication. Concrete symbols that represent and physically resemble what they are, are used to communicate. Concrete symbols move feel or sound like what they are. They can be pictures, but can also be objects (a shoelace to represent 'shoe'), iconic gestures (such as patting a chair to say "sit down"), and sounds, such as buzzing to sound like a bee. Typically developing children use concrete symbols in conjunction with words and gestures, generally between 12 and 24 months.

For some users the transition from tangible objects to symbol pictures may be the use of tangible object-based icons. These are photos or drawings that have been laminated and cut out into the shape of the actual thing. They can be easily Velcro'd to a felt board or Velcro-covered page. These are also often used when working with books with students who need symbols to tell about or participate in a retell of the story. Illustrations from the book are copied, laminated, and used as manipulatives to tell the story.

Photographs of specific places, events, or people are often used at this stage.

Typically developing children at this level, between 18 and 24 months, may have as many as 300 words. Given the same communicative intents, examples of vocabulary can include:

> a ball, this ball, that ball
>
> no ball, no more juice, juice all gone
>
> more juice, more swing
>
> no
>
> big ball, dirty ball, broken truck
>
> daddy car, my nose, doggy ear
>
> read a book, ride this
>
> away ball, up me

In the next phase of development both functions and syntax expand.

Level 6. Abstract symbols: This includes speech, signs, Braille or printed words used to communicate. These symbols are abstract because they are not physically similar to what they represent. They are used one at a time. This typically occurs between 12 and 24 months. This is when typically developing children start to use words consistently, building their vocabulary as they share using words with others. This is where deaf children in a deaf community begin using signs consistently to communicate with others in their community. All words - either spoken or written - are abstract symbols. It is not possible to detect their meaning by looking at them. They do not resemble what they represent.

This is, ideally, the point at which AAC users should begin growing their vocabulary of symbol use. AAC systems should contain symbols that are used consistently with and by partners. AAC users at this stage should already have a robust symbol system that partners have been using to provided aided input, and should be using these symbols themselves, slowly building vocabulary with practice and feedback.

Level 7. Language: Symbols (both concrete and abstract) are combined into two or three symbol combinations ("want juice," "me go out") according to grammatical rules. The individual understands that the meaning of symbol combinations may differ depending upon how the symbols are ordered. Typically, this begins around 24 months.

Moving Beyond Requesting

Depending upon the type of AAC system provided and the amount of Aided Language Stimulation effected in the environment, AAC users may already be developing a variety of communication functions. However, this is not always the case. Too often intervention plans focus on requesting and rejecting and stop there, having met the user's basic needs.

Just a quick look at the aforementioned behaviors can tell us that requesting and rejecting don't meet all communication needs. Individuals have a need to tell us when they are uncomfortable and unhappy, when something is wrong, when someone is bothering them, when they feel good about something, and more. Making an intervention plan that looks at the individual's day, the types of communication his peers are using at each of the segments or activities of the day, and determining where he is unable to approach the same provides invaluable information for AAC planning.

There are a few basic reasons to communicate that span a wide variety of intents and message types. Children communicate to indicate a preference or desire, to make a choice, to request an object or activity/action, to comment, to share, to request information or escape or attention. They might also use language to make up stories, to assert their independence, and to express feelings. The key is to have language available for them to use in any of these situations and to make sure that the symbols they need are easily accessed.

Pull out or Push in:

This is often a loaded question, and one that almost always provokes very strong reactions. Many parents still believe that their child isn't getting the full benefit of intervention if it's not 1:1 with the SLP. Many teachers still do not want speech-language pathologists in their classroom. Many SLPs are still far more comfortable with traditional intervention activities than in teaming up with teachers in classrooms.

Remember; you can't teach language in discrete trial training. (Lovaas 1992) You can build skills and develop vocabulary in therapeutic interventions, but language must be developed in natural contexts. Too often the AAC system is separate from the context or activity. Rather, AAC use needs to be infused into play and other leisure or motivating activities. At any level of intervention, the partner needs to respond to the user's communicative intent, expand on the message appropriately with both speech and AAC, and to continue providing meaningful opportunities within the activity to communicate. By definition, then, intervention is not best provided in 1:1 formats.

Communication must always have a purpose. And it must be motivating at least a good deal of the time. Beginning with AAC learning by responding to curriculum questions or demands in a task or activity that is not interesting often results in the AAC user shutting down. Intervention targets can focus on vocabulary, or syntax, or pragmatics or operational competence, but it must focus on keeping the AAC learner engaged.

To increase social communication skills, you need to have a group. It is very difficult to increase social language skills in a 1:1 session. Peers need to interact with each other in typical ways. Create classroom or group sessions that simulate typical settings; such as going to the store, a party, or a "play date." Provide opportunities to interact in real life situations in which the AAC learned is interested. Create opportunities for learning routines, for learning the language needed within the routine, for learning how to regulate behavior and use appropriate language responses.

Intervention Sessions

Preparing adapted activities that include appropriate visual cues and motivating topics, does take a little extra time and thought. In speech-language therapy a lot of time is spent increasing vocabulary skills. This can be done through book reading, use of thematic units, concept mapping, and a variety of other explicit instruction techniques. All of these apply to AAC users as well. They are particularly important to AAC users who may not have had the same life experiences as their peers. Remember, vocabulary knowledge is second only to decoding in importance in developing reading skills. And all students need to develop literacy skills.

Some therapists create real-life situations in therapy sessions in order to practice vocabulary with students. That may include setting up a pretend birthday party in order to learn not only the vocabulary related to birthday parties, but also the social conventions, the way to interact with others at a party, how to relate to the person having the birthday and receiving the gifts, how to handle not being the one getting gifts, taking turns in games, asking for things politely, etc.

Use existing classroom and intervention session routines to also give a context for social language; such as greetings and partings, social manners, conversing during breaks. Use class and session routines to create scripts that can be used over and over again. Teach the AAC user what he needs to say to direct the actions of others, to gain others' attention, to provide information, to direct or explain routines. To tell about things or events.

Teach AAC users how to participate in classroom and home tasks. This is especially important when classroom tasks are a group or class of activity that will be repeated throughout the classroom experience. Remember that this is a process. The end product is the AAC user's communication, and nothing else.

For more decontextualized intervention, therapists can create materials that provide multiple opportunities to practice target skills. The key is to remember that any activity used for verbal students who require language intervention can be used with students who need AAC.

One of the things heard the most often from speech-language pathologists in the schools is that they don't have enough time to program dynamic display devices. Too often they are asked - or think they need - to program page after page of curriculum content, story details, activity specific vocabulary for each AAC user on their caseload.

This is where the notions of core vocabulary, activity boards, and descriptive teaching come in handy, as well as methods of introducing temporary vocabulary into the AAC system for specific short-term use. When using core word systems, minimal programing is needed, as the words used by the learner with this system can be used to make a wide variety of responses and message types/formats for most situations.

Fringe vocabulary can be added permanently as flip book additions to the system, or on individual boards made for specific topics used for the short-term. With the PODD and other types of communication books,

Post-its are handy for temporarily adding vocabulary to a book that may not be needed long-term.

Therapy time can include systematic introduction of specific vocabulary and syntactic structures in therapeutic format, generalization to classroom, home, and other environments, as well as looking at responding to the curriculum differently. Choosing and introducing vocabulary becomes key. You may not make a PODD book for every student (although that would be good). You may not have an AAC device for every AAC user (although that, too, would be good). But if you at least provide a basic core vocabulary with even 1 word per function, you've given that student more ability to communicate than 20 nouns. You should include at least 1 word per major communicative function, key people/places, and the verbs, adjectives and prepositions with the broadest applications.

Goals should include increasing the number of language functions; including mediating/regulating (getting help, directing others) and discussing/describing (commenting, questioning). Being able to produce messages (even the simplest construction) for different intents is a major accomplishment.

Remember to work closely with the child's team. You are all important members of the AAC user's team. Engineering the environment so that there are multiple opportunities to practice each target function, construction, word is important, and it must be consistent across environments for the student to learn to use it. Make those 200 opportunities each day happen. (Musselwhite)

The importance of stability of vocabulary for learning and that implication for intervention cannot be over-stressed. It is not always necessary to drill discrimination of the symbol. Many students learn to use symbols without ever identifying them in isolation. They learn by motor patterns. If the vocabulary is always in the same location many students can get there without even looking; via motor automaticity.

Consistent location and repetition are the keys to learning, not necessarily visual discrimination. And if you are consistently providing aided language input, using the symbols along with your verbal input, the students will learn what the symbols mean without needing isolated discrimination drills.

"This child's communication book/board has too many pictures, it's too distracting, I know he needs a lot of vocabulary, but sometimes I can't teach it with so much there."

This is a time to use masking. Cover up some words (many devices have hidden keys options to 'hide' some buttons during learning phases). Then the focus can be on target words, and learners will reduce random selections or mis-hits.

A time saving tip for AAC intervention comes from Gayle Porter. Make the communication page or board as big as the AAC learner will be using in the long run. This doesn't need to be forever, but should be beyond the next short-term objective. Paper masks can then be used to cover some words. By cutting parts of the mask away as needed the need to keep re-making the board, book, or page is obviated. On high-tech devices it is much easier to hide and reveal keys than re-program the whole page. And much easier for the AAC learner to learn where the buttons are located and not need to re-learn as his vocabulary grows.

The Take-Away:

Effective Intervention = providing structured opportunities to communicate.

- Students with complex communication needs must receive numerous highly structured opportunities; incidental opportunities are not effective for acquisition of new forms.

- Structured opportunities for communication should include at least:

  discriminative stimulus: what you do or say to elicit a response

response: what you want the student to do (may be prompted initially)

consequence: what you do to reinforce the response

- These discreet trials are effective, do not need to be provided in isolation (should not be provided in isolation), should be integrated into the context of daily routines by everyone working with the students. Therapists and teachers should work with families and everyone interacting with the student to increase generalization of communication targets.

Romski, M. A., Sevcik, R. A., Cheslock, M., & Barton, A. (2006). The System for Augmenting Language: AAC and Emerging Language Intervention. In R. McCauley & M. Fey (Eds). Treatment of Language Disorders in Children. Baltimore: Paul H. Brookes.

Chapter 7
Literacy

"The idea is to give kids as many AAC learning opportunities across contexts as possible. I'd argue that you teach reading to AAC users the same way you teach any kid — balance, balance, balance." (Koppenhaver, 2008)

While it is not within the scope of this book to explain how to teach AAC users literacy skills, I did want to briefly touch on it; because I think it is critical that we teach AAAC users how to read, and that both parents and SLPs know how to approach the skills.

Literacy skills are needed for academic, social, and access to most employment (Musselwhite). But most AAC users don't acquire literacy skills. This is not because they can't, but because many are not taught.

Robinson & Soto (2011) ask, "Why do AAC users struggle with literacy?" Their answer is that AAC users have:

- limited expressive speech to develop sound articulation
- difficulty with verbal memory and low phonemic awareness
- comprehension problems
- limited access to materials

- limited opportunities for interaction through text

- and lack of direct instruction.

They take us back to Cunningham's 4 Blocks Literacy instruction as a way to teach AAC users; not just general education students. There are difficulties with this, as the authors point out. In particular, AAC users have limited experiences for building background knowledge and vocabulary.

Research has shown us that students with disabilities learn literacy skills in much the same sequence as typical peers. All students need to develop phonemic awareness, phonics skills and sight word knowledge, reading fluency or word processing, vocabulary comprehension and reading text comprehension.

It is imperative that careful thought and attention be given to the specific reading instructional materials and strategies presented to the student. The student's physical and sensory skills, linguistic skills and cognitive skills all need to be factored into the presentation of every task, as well as expectations. Unfortunately, any student's limitations in physical movements, fatigue, cortical vision impairment will contribute to difficulties with accessing print. Use of page turners, OCRs, screen readers, enlarged print with contrasting colors, constant assessment of presentation location and angle, and consistent presentation of opportunities to interact with stories are all pieces of his literacy and language program. Additionally, the fact that the student is learning to build language skills at the same time he is learning to build literacy skills needs to be considered.

The effort needed to develop literacy and language simultaneously is huge. The student needs to be fully engaged and motivated by his activities in order for him to take away from them. Social interaction may be a big motivator for some, and maximizing the opportunities for students to work with a partner or as a part of a group would then be important. But within each of these situations the student needs to be presented with materials with which he can engage as independently as possible.

It is also imperative that language development and literacy development be carefully intertwined in this instruction. For example, consistent use of a repeated reading shared reading strategy with multiple language-based purposes for reading/listening, followed by specific language-based activities and literacy foundations and writing tasks are important. Immerse the student in as many literacy activities as possible. Read. Read. And read some more. Create a print rich environment. Encourage predicting what will happen next. Encourage commenting about the text and illustrations. Encourage asking questions about the text. Even encourage labeling. Encourage creation of personal books. These can be as simple and pasting photos onto paper and writing a line under each. Or you can use storybook apps or websites (such as www.tarheelreader.org).

Evidence based practice calls for 90 minutes of reading instruction per day for general education students. Add to that an additional 30-60 minutes per day for struggling readers. But how many AAC users get 2-3 hours per day of reading instruction? Research is relatively new on EBP reading instruction for students who use AAC.

One thing we do know is that we should read - all the time, a variety of interesting stories on a variety of topics, and a variety of types of text. Musselwhite and King-DeBaun originally talked about 2 types of books; books for literacy and language learning, and books for enjoyment or enrichment. But we usually break text into 3 types; including:

- Enrichment books that you read to the child. These are rich in graphics, develop background knowledge for topics, support learning concepts, and have a variety of vocabulary and sentence types. These are books for enjoyment, but also for enrichment and building experiences with words.

- Transition books that have fewer illustrations and whose text students can often read by themselves. These books move children into early literacy participation, particularly when there is repetition of a line.

- Conventional text for students to read themselves, which contain many high frequency words students have learned already.

Readings of enrichment texts should be interactive to get students engaged, and to teach them that print carries meaning. The pictures should support the print, but not carry meaning.

Read these books all the time, and read a variety of different types of enrichment books. Talking about stories encourages thinking and language skills, and facilitates reading comprehension. Reading to students is EBP for developing literacy and language skills when adults provide mediation and scaffolding (Erickson).

Reading to students provides motivation for them to want to learn to read. It teaches them about purposes for reading. It provides experience with books they can't read independently. And it gives a sense of the meaningfulness of written language.

According to Carol Westby (2009) rehearsal and retelling of stories is important in the development of language and literacy skills in children. Children with Complex Communication Needs (CNN) don't get this experience; impacting their language and literacy development. Typically developing children begin 1st grade with a 6,000-word spoken vocabulary. (Montgomery, 2008) How many words can our AAC users use?

Before - During - After strategy

Researchers (Erickson, Koppenhaver, Yoder) have encouraged us to use the same Before-During-After framework that is used in general education.

Before reading, activate prior knowledge about the topic, pre-teach concepts, find topical words in the AAC system, and practice a specific type of comprehension strategy to be used after reading.

For example, if the book is about a trip to the zoo, the Before activity might be to find the zoo animals in the AAC system (verbal students can just name them). Or it might be to sort zoo animals v. not zoo animals. If the After activity will be to compare/contrast two zoo animals, then start by comparing two students or two items in the classroom.

Set the purpose for reading. You might tell the child to listen for all the animals the characters saw at the zoo, or for the description of one animal.

During reading, name the animals in the illustrations as you see them in the story. Ask questions, such as; "They're going to the reptile house. What do you think they will find there?"

After reading, engage students in a task that matches the purpose set for reading. If you focused on comparing two things before reading, then choose two of the animals in the book and compare and contrast them, based on the text and the illustrations.

Story maps are a standard of literacy instruction. For our AAC users, it provides them with a visual structure to the story, allows them to use pictures to express what they know, and it allows the AAC user to tell/retell the story. (See examples in Appendix).

Story narratives are also used to develop language skills. There are structural similarities between personal narratives (which tell about a specific personal experience) and story re-telling (which tells a specific story, usually fictional). Students learn topic maintenance, event sequencing, use of elaboration and the need for fluency.

You can prime AAC users for retelling a story by having them practice telling the steps of a routine or the sequence of events in an activity. Use first - next - last icons, or a numbered sequence and/or use icons for the story elements.

There are semantic mapping strategies (showing how words are related) that can help teach the students the words in the story they don't already know. They can learn what type of word it is, what it's related to, what category it is in, where it is in their AAC system.

Vocabulary that can be targeted in reading includes synonyms/antonyms, associations, categories, referential definitions and, of course, core words. Practice vocabulary while describing characters in the story, having students describe themselves; compare and contrast themselves with the character, compare and contrast characters from two similar stories, describe the setting in a story, describe where they live, compare and contrast the settings from two different stories.

After reading, follow up the activity they were primed for. Use the vocabulary in the AAC system to describe 1 animal, or compare/contrast 2 characters, or describe the setting, or list the character traits of one character.

Use story maps to provide visual cues, to allow the AAC user to express what they know, and allow the AAC user to retell the story. Prime AAC users for retelling events in a story by having them practice sequencing steps to a familiar task; such as a bedtime routine, the meals in a day, or the steps of a routine task. Use first - next - last icons, use a number sequence, use icons for the story elements.

Adapted story re-tellings (or independent reenactments) are necessary for building skills (DeBaun 2010, Westby 2009). Children gain confidence in reading skills by retelling stories to friends, parents, siblings, stuffed animals, pets. AAC users don't get this practice with fluent telling. They miss practicing vocabulary and syntax. Giving them symbol supports to re-tell stories increases their engagement with books, increases their opportunities to practice language and increases expressive language through books. This activity increases language, but not necessarily literacy.

To build literacy skills we need to build in text and fade out symbols. Transitional readers get opportunities to re-tell stories with story-specific displays independently. As we add in sight words, we focus on the words. As we separate text from symbols, we encourage use of text in the book and symbols in the AAC system. If you must keep symbols in the book, keep them on the bottom of the page for discussion purposes.

Adapt your teaching procedures to eliminate the need for a spoken response. Students can choose from a selection of symbols, words, or letters; either in the AAC system on a separate communication board, or even on 3x5 cards. Provide an oral model while encouraging internal subvocalization. Provide an adapted version of the story during the read-aloud, or use a story kit. Give the child a symbol to hold up each time he hears a target word. Give the student props to use to re-enact the story. Have the child match a picture to one in the book. Have the student fill in a line using their AAC system in a Cloze activity (fill in the blank).

What constitutes our literacy instruction? There are 3 prongs to our attack on literacy skills:

1. Vocabulary and story structure (which we've just been talking about),

2. Sight words, and

3. Phonological, phonemic, & phonological awareness

Phonological awareness skills are one's comprehension or awareness of the sound structure of language. Torgeson et al, defined it as the "...ability to notice, to think about, and manipulate phonemes of words..." They are necessary but not sufficient for building reading skills. If the student doesn't also have vocabulary comprehension, the words are meaningless. And, as we've said, our AAC users frequently don't get the same experiences - which build vocabulary - as their peers. Vocabulary plays a huge role in reading skills. When children with CCN (complex communication needs) don't get the same vocabulary input and don't get the experiences, then they don't "get" reading.

Often literacy intervention for AAC users is minimal and focused on sight words and further instruction, even if attempted, may be stuck due to lack of vocabulary. So, we need to keep teaching language; especially vocabulary skills. And our instruction needs to be engaging, interactive, meaningful, and repetitive.

Most reading comprehension failures in general are due to a lack of language comprehension, not always the inability to "read" the words. Students' knowledge of vocabulary, semantic relationships, morphological and syntactic structures are often too limited. Their exposure both in context and in class are limited; certainly, much more limited than their neurotypical peers.

- Typical students can learn new words incidentally. Most of our AAC users need explicit instruction.

- Typical students understand vocabulary through experiences. But again, many students with disabilities don't have the same experiences.

- Typical students learn phonological awareness and phonemic awareness skills. These skills are often not taught to AAC users.

We need to change the perception in others that the child who can't speak has nothing to say. Or that the child who can't move consistently can't be taught to respond. Or that the nonspeaking child cannot be taught to read when he cannot say the letter sounds or words himself.

We need to build understanding in the child of the sound structure of language, and the ability to manipulate sounds in words. We need to teach letter-sound correspondence, rhyme and word families, and recognition of visual patterns.

Sometimes we just use literature to build language skills. But even the simplest read aloud session helps to demonstrate emergent literacy skills to children; which way is up, how do I hold the book, where is the front, when do I turn the page?

Light and McNaughton list 5 types of instructional content we should be providing students with CCN, which roughly correlate with the 3 prongs of instruction with which I started. These include:

1. Reading interesting texts of all types to students.

2. Building language skills.

3. Teaching Phonological Awareness skills, letter/sound correspondence, and single word decoding.

4. Engaging students in shared reading activities

5. Providing experiences with early writing.

Reading to students is everyone's first recommendation for building language and literacy skills. Try to relate the topic of the story to the students' own lives. Encourage them to ask questions, give opinions, make comments, fill in a blank at the end of a sentence.

AAC users need vocabulary, syntax, and morphology. Understanding beyond transitional books requires comprehension of complex sentences.

Light & McNaughton also list 4 components of instruction:

1. Phonological awareness: Segmenting words, blending sounds, letter/sound correspondence, decoding, early writing. Adults should use a Model -> Prompt -> strategy (or Demonstrate -> guided practice, -> check).

2. Maximize the AAC user's exposure to literacy instruction and book reading.

3. Fade your scaffolding/support.

4. Incorporate books into every day experiences and use the student's own experiences to make books meaningful.

Using their program, we can eliminate the need for a spoken response for AAC users in Phonological Awareness activities. Their research has found the 2 most important or relevant areas in Phonological Awareness to work on with students are initial phoneme segmentation and sound blending. These 2 skills are the most highly correlated with future literacy success. Their literacy program (available at the Penn State website) focuses on 3 tasks, all of which use between 2-5 choices which are named as they are put out:

• matching the target phoneme presented orally to a picture,

- blending 3 phonemes, and

- letter/sound correspondence.

They recommend teaching using lower case letters, as these are encountered the most by students. They also recommend beginning with the most commonly used consonants: /b/, /d/, /m/, /n/, and with short vowels before long.

Once sound blending skills are consistent and the student knows 5-6 letters/sounds correspondences they recommend working on simple decoding. Build up automaticity with words learned, so that the student can reduced the cognitive load needed for text passages using those words.

Put out 4 similar pictures (Light & McNaughton suggest [map, mop, mat, nap]. When the student sees the word, he picks the picture. After this, the student can practice in simple readers and with Cloze procedures (fill in the blank).

Beginning with simple readers means students don't have to put a strain on the cognitive load needed to keep track of story elements. We can keep the use of repetitive lines and sentence starters. As story grammar develops then we can teach familiar story schemes so that students can "write" their own books.

We can have students find the two words that begin with the same sound, or end with the same rhyme, or which words in the story begin with (sound). We can have students listen in the story and then find the word in their AAC system that had the same ending sound. And we can have them clap the number of syllables in words from the story. And, the beauty of a robust AAC system is that you do not need to program all of these words into the system. They are already there (if you have a robust system).

For example: "What word rhymes with shoe?" "Blue." Ok, blue is a color. Where are the color words in your AAC system?"

<u>For example</u>: "Find as many _at words as you can." "Good; cat, rat, and bat are all _at words. They are all [animals]. You can find them on the animals' pages. Hat is also an _at word. Where will it be?" "Hat is something you wear. Where are the clothing pages?" "Fat is an _at word. Find it in the ___ pages." (Describing.)

Phonological skills are necessary, but not sufficient. Decoding is irrelevant if you don't know the word's meaning. Which brings us back to vocabulary again.

Let's go back to the 3 types of text we read to kids.

1. Enrichment books; rich in graphics and text. They develop background knowledge, support learning concepts, and have a variety of vocabulary and sentence types. These are the books you read to children in an interactive activity that keeps them engaged. Pictures in these stories should support the print, but not carry the whole meaning of the print.

   Enrichment books are for use in shared reading and in core curriculum content. Book displays (specific communication board or page) made specifically for a topic or book might provide a mode of content-specific participation, but students typically cannot sequence symbols in these to construct messages.

   Instead, give students activities that give access to comprehension; that is, Before-During-After activities with multiple purposes for reading that allow for interactive participation and building vocabulary. It is suggested that literacy success for these complex communicators is dependent on interaction between these students and their more competent peers. (King-DeBaun)

   When adapting these books, don't over-use symbols. We want to preserve the importance of text for meaning and the 1:1 correspondence of printed symbol to spoken word.

   Begin with symbol supports that match the text, including any sight words. Since verbal children get lots of opportunities to "read" books they've heard dozens of times, they get the opportunity to practice far more than their nonspeaking peers.

AAC users don't get this same experience with successful interactions with text.

2. Transition books are used when students are beginning to use some strategies to read unknown words. The focus is on the text, not on the graphics. These books look simple; students can read them independently. They contain repeated lines and few words per page, they use rhyme, rhythm, and repetition; and they use some graphics to text support. There is a close picture/text match.

   These books are used to focus on reader strategies; looking at the initial sound, the word length, and picture cues. Simple repeated text structures lead to successful opportunities with print.

   Students reading transitional books should know most letters of the alphabet most of the time and should recognize signs and logos. These students get stuck somewhere between story retelling with symbols and silent reading. Once a student can re-tell the story after 4-5 re-tellings, they no longer need the symbol support.

   Transitional books can be programed into AAC systems; the repetitive line can go on a BigMack button, sequences of story lines and be programed into a Sequencer button. This allows for participation, not just passive presence. But it does not develop story and sentence structure, so don't get stuck here. To program a display that allows students to "read" "Brown Bear, Brown Bear" would require the user to product 5-7 hits on the display to read any page.

   Separate the symbols from the text, King-DeBaun suggests. Text goes at the top of the page; symbols go at the bottom. This helps students to learn that text or words are for reading and the symbols are for communicating. When we use symbols on a specific display, we are asking students to communicate; not read. Our AAC users need both practice communication and practice reading.

   If a student can retell a story after 4-5 readings, then the symbol supports are no longer necessary. If we've also been teaching this AAC user core words, then they have the reusable words they need to construct messages and responses. These developing readers have some minimal literacy skills, but often get stuck here.

What strategies does King-DeBaun find necessary? Her list is slightly different from Light & McNaughton's.

- Learning Core words and sight words

- Learn how to find them in the AAC system

- Speak the text with AAC

- Put the word on a Word Wall

- Spell it

3. Conventional texts look easy. They are for students who can use word reading strategies to read unknown words. Instruction at this point minimizes the scaffolds provided by rhyme and repetition. These stories are short and use a lot of high frequency words. Students can read them once they have 50-75 sight words.

Adapting reading instruction for students who use AAC can take different strategies. One way phonological awareness activities have been adapted is in the literacy program developed by Light and McNaughton, (2014). The activities of phoneme blending, initial sound identification, and rhyme are adapted so that the mode of response is a picture symbol selection.

Ogden Nash and Jack Prelutsky are both good poets to use in these tasks. Or construct your own poems and tongue twisters.

What core words do we find or use in shared reading activities? Core words for reading books can include: want, go, more, again, help, not that, want different, read more, look, see, read, all done, good, bad, funny, sad, he, she, it, now, where is...? favorite, who, what do?

Importance of Shared Reading:

Shared reading is usually done with beginning readers, as a way to provide access to a variety of literature, and to instill a love of reading. Studies recommended that children be read to at least 15 minutes per day.

When the adult thinks out loud during read aloud sessions they model for students how to deal with unfamiliar vocabulary and concepts. Adults need to model strategies in order for students to learn to use them. Prediction is particularly important; stop throughout the story to predict what might happen next. Prediction questions increase comprehension.

For students in special education who are just developing literacy skills shared reading time is an important tool for increasing background knowledge and language. Shared reading is not about the student learning how to answer questions; it is about developing a love of reading and beginning to use emergent reading skills. Adults need to recognize that students may ask questions repeatedly during the session; often repeating the same questions repeatedly. This is because they are learning language; they may build understanding of your response a little at a time (Erickson). Students should eventually be turning pages, "reading" repeated lines, making comments, and asking questions.

One of the objectives of shared reading is to connect the content of the book to experiences the student has had and the background knowledge he has obtained. One strategy for this is to follow the C-A-R (washingtonlearningsystems.org), which directs us to start with a **Comment**, then wait 10-15 seconds. **Ask** for participation, then stop and wait for 10-15 seconds. **Respond** by repeating and adding more to the student's response.

While reading pause to identify objects and actions; ask about characters, objects, and events; and make comments. Model asking questions using the device: "Who is (doing action)?" "Who is (descriptor)" "Who is (location)?" "Where is (character, object)?" "What is (character) doing?"

Stories increase vocabulary; but they also increase understanding of story grammar, narrative skills, and syntax. Narrative teaching strategies are just as useful for teaching picture or text-based language as they are for students using oral language - if not more so. Because students can become interested in the problems of the story/movie/T.V. show's characters; stories become a natural medium for learning language.

Narrative teaching strategies for stories include (but are not limited to) compare/contrast diagrams, thinking activities, episode maps and story maps, journals, internal states maps, semantic word maps, story retellings, summarizing, and story generating. (You will find templates for these in the Appendix)

Retelling the story can be done a number of different ways; depending on the student's skills and needs for modification.

1. Make sentence strips that, together, retell the story. Keep them simple and use a single symbol as a visual cue.

2. Make pictures of each story element and action - again in summary - for students to put in order.

3. Make a word/symbol bank of core words and specific fringe for the story. Students use these to retell the story.

4. Create simple sentence or symbol strips; have vocals symbols for describing words. Students tell the story with more complex vocabulary.

Studies have suggested that shared reading should be done at least 15 minutes per day - which is really not very much. But many of our AAC users don't even get this much. If a child is not interested in sitting still for this time span, try reading with a book on tape or an animated book on a tablet.

When I'm working with students who use AAC I am also focused on having them learn how to find the words in their AAC system that they need to talk about the book. If the book is about a trip to the zoo, we'll look for zoo animals in the AAC system, and for animals that do NOT belong to the group "zoo animals," and we'll describe and contrast these animals.

Some examples for you:

Where the Wild Things Are

Somebody (who) - Max

Wanted (problem) - to be with the Wild Things

But (problem) - he missed his home/Mom

So (solution/resolution) - sailed back home

Story elements: (with pictures)

people	place	things actions adjectives
Max (high) bad	home	jump
Mom loud	island	run
Wild Things		yell

While reading:

- Pause to identify objects and actions

- Ask about characters and objects

- Make comments

The communication partner (cp) models, using the AAC system,

- Who is (doing action)?

- Who is (color, other descriptor)?

- Who is (location)?

- Where is (character, object)?

- What is (character) doing?

Narrative teaching strategies are just as useful for reaching picture or text-based language strategies as they are for students using oral language (if not more so). Because students become interested in the problems of story (movie, t.v). characters, stories become a natural medium for learning language.

Narrative teaching strategies for stories include (but are not limited to):

- compare/contrast diagrams

- thinking activities

- episode maps and story maps

- journals

- internal-states charts

- semantic word maps

- story re-tellings

- summarizing

- story generating

The same strategies use for oral students apply to AAC users:

- referencing the text: "Look at the boy running."

- Cloze procedure: "The boy is __"

- expansion: "Yes, the boy is running."

- binary choice: "Is the boy sitting or running?"

- modeling: only in this case, pointing to picture symbols in the AAC system rather than verbal models only

- open ended question: "What is the boy doing?"

What usually prevents AAC users from participating in these activities is a lack of vocabulary in the AAC system.

Fireflies by **Julie Brinckloe**

Before reading: discuss whether students have ever seen a firefly and describe them. Ask if they've ever caught them in a jar. What happened?

Set the purpose for reading: Think about what the sky looked like with all the fireflies in it. Think about how the boy felt at the end of the story. What did he do? Why?

During the story: pause when he gets the jar and ask what they think he will do with it. If they don't know, ask again when the boy puts the holes in the lid of the jar.

After reading, have students:

Describe what the sky looked like with all the fireflies in it. "The fireflies made the sky look ___ "

Describe how the boy felt when he caught them. "He felt ___ "

Describe how the boy felt when he went to bed. "He felt ___ "

Why do you think he let them go? "He wanted them to be able to ___ "

Can you think of any other animals that light up?

Only use the cloze procedure if students can't generate responses on their own. Have students re-tell the story by using and ordering sentence strips with some visual cues. The degree of visual support will change depending on each student.

Other activities within a story:

- match describing words (i.e. The jars were -> dusty, The fireflies were -> bright)

- sequencing the story with pictures (Strega Nona waned help. Anthony applied. She said not to touch the pot).

- copy the pictures in the book of the characters (you can do this for a book you own in order to make it accessible to a student(s) with difficulty accessing text). Laminate the images and staple to popsicle sticks. Distribute among students and have them hold up their character when they appear in the story, or to respond to a question.

- make a story map

The Girl Who Loved Wild Horses by **Paul Goble**

Before: Look in the AAC system to find animals that are wild, tame.

During: Find the words in the "describing words" section of the AAC system to tell what these words mean: "… prancing to-and- fro," "His eyes shone like cold stars," and "… a mane and tail floating like wisps clouds about her.."

After:

- Divide the book into its several episodes and summarized the key words of each.

- Make picture supports and have students sort the pictures into their correct episodes

- Have students find the words in their AAC systems to tell about each episode (thunderstorms, horse jumping/rearing up, girl rides horse, they get lost, they are frightened)

The Island of the Blue Dolphins by **Scott O'Dell**

Who: Kana, Chief, Russians, Tutok, Ramo

Did What, Why: battle, make canoe, came in ships

Where: island, cave, rock pool, village

When: Ending: Mission

Example: The Snowy Day by **Ezra Jack Keats**

Vocabulary: drag, hit, throw, cold, white, wet

Sequence: what Peter did outside, what Peter did inside

Phonological Awareness: find words that rhyme with 'snow,' find words that begin with the same sound as 'winter'

_OW; match the initial letters/sounds to the rime pictures (using symbols); THR, M, SN, BL

Vocabulary: describe how Peter felt outside, describe how the snowy world looked, what happened to the snowball

Compare/Contrast: make a Venn diagram comparing/contrasting Winter where you live and Winter where Peter lives

Vocabulary: find all the weather words in your AAC system (temperature, cold, etc.).

Story Grammar:

1. Somebody: Peter

2. Wanted: to save a snowball (keep)

3. But: it melted

4. So: he was sad.

Or: Story Pyramid:

A. Peter
B. Cold, White
C. Boy, Small, Happy
D. He made snow angels

E. He hit tree with stick

Explicit Vocabulary Instruction: More activities to teach vocabulary

Use all of the same vocabulary activities you are already using with your speaking students/children. Sometimes you will want to highlight key core words, but don't forget that AAC users need more than basic core.

Make vocabulary cards and

- play card games; such as Go Fish-style, Old Maid-style, and Memory-style

- do matching activities for synonyms and antonyms, then ask students why they go together

- make a deck of cards that list items within a category; student identifies the category on the AAC system

- make a deck of cards with objects; student tells about its texture or color or another attribute on their AAC system, make BINGO cards to turn this into a game for receptive language

- make BINGO-type cards with thematic vocabulary; instead of calling out the label, call out a description or definition and students determines what the word is before putting a marker on it. You can have the student find the item in the AAC system first. A few examples: occupation BINGO, furniture BINGO, food BINGO, community places BINGO, appliance BINGO - any topic your student need to add vocabulary for.

King-DeBaun and Erickson (2006) emphasize the point that the objective is not to have a parallel program running for students in the class who are included. The point, they say, is to have a single instructional strategy that works for all students, with differentiation. They point out:

1. Include all students in any whole class instruction. They need to participate; not just be present in the room.

2. Use struggling readers groups for all struggling readers; not just included students; and don't do it during independent reading times. These students need that time, as well.

3. Model computer use for the whole class; for taking notes, written responses, etc. - so that this is not just a strategy for the AAC user.

4. Model communication board/device use for the whole class. AAC users need lots and lots of models of others using AAC to respond, ask, etc. It helps all students to clarify directions visually; not just auditorily input. The authors also point out that by having us use the child's AAC system, it is much easier to find where that system falls to meet our needs.

5. In any group instruction, call on everyone when possible. Establish a simple response for students with physical disabilities in advance, so they can participate in answering questions.

6. Use PAS (partner assisted scanning) with all students to establish comprehension. Other struggling students will really benefit, too.

7. Use 1st letter cues. If a student with a communication impairment doesn't have the words they need to use, the 1st letter cue can be a strategy. This is, again, a strategy that communication partners can model.

There are, then, 3 things we can all do to help AAC users develop literacy skills:

1. Read to them. With good read aloud and shared reading strategies we can build background knowledge, comprehension, and vocabulary skills. Read a variety of different types of text on different topics. And re-read books multiple times, so that students can get to the stage of retelling or "reading" the books themselves.

2. Develop Phonological Awareness skills. Create specific structured activities for teaching rhyme, sound identification and manipulations, phoneme and syllable segmentation, sound blending.

3. Continue to teach sight words; but not as the only component of literacy instruction. Create a word wall that works specifically for your student(s).

In the appendix you will find specific examples as well as a template for planning your own shared reading and phonological awareness activities.

Phonological Awareness

- recognize and produce rhyming words

- count, pronounce, blend, and segment syllables in words

- blend and segment onset and rimes for 1-syllable words

- isolate initial, medial vowel, and final sounds in CVC words

- add or substitute individual sounds in CVC words to make new words

Phonics

- demonstrate understanding of 1:1 letter/sound correspondence

- associate long and short sounds with graphemes for 5 major vowels

- read high frequency words on sight

- distinguish between similarly spelled words by identifying the letter sounds that are different

CHAPTER 8

Special Populations

By the end of this section, the learner will be able to:

- Explain the impact of cerebral palsy on AAC considerations

- Define cortical vision impairment (CVI) and list at least 3 ways to adapt picture communication systems and access modes to accommodate it

- Describe the impact of Rett Syndrome on communication access and considerations for AAC systems

- List 4 alternate access modes for individuals who cannot use direct selection

- Explain why AAC might be considered for children with developmental dyspraxia/apraxia of speech

- Discuss the benefits of using AAC with individuals with Autism Spectrum Disorder (ASD)

Cerebral Palsy:

No doubt if you're the parent of a child with C.P. you are well aware of the symptoms and complexities, so I won't re-state them here. Cotter,

Carter, and Porter (2008) delineate some key issues for participating in learning for individuals with cerebral palsy, which apply to use of AAC:

- Associated Reactions: those involuntary movements of head, mouth, neck, trunk, extremities that happen during voluntary movement which the individual needs to learn to disassociate

- Symmetry: individuals with cerebral palsy almost always show a degree of asymmetry of the body; using both sides of the body is often must be learned

- Weight-Bearing: opportunities to bear weight on arms or legs may be missing due to atypical tone to motor development and as a result muscles, muscle strength, and joint strength are not fully developed. Opportunities for weight-bearing must be provided throughout the day

- Weight Shift: the ability to shift weight and maintain stability is necessary, for example, for moving their hand or using a switch

- Gravity Effects: individuals with cerebral palsy may be unable to counteract the impact of gravity by using their muscles to maintain positions; they may fatigue easily due to the effort this takes

- Stability: individuals with cerebral palsy may have difficulty with strengthening the head, trunk, neck, shoulders, and hips in order to move extremities to perform tasks, or with using opening and grasping of hands to stabilize the arms in order to move the body; this needs to be learned

- Fatigue: is the effect on the body of maintaining stability, countering the impact of gravity, bearing and shifting weight, controlling associated reactions, and controlling movements. Fatigue happens much faster for individuals with cerebral palsy. Activities need to be paced, and to involve less concentrated effort by the afternoon. Individuals may shut down for periods to recuperate.

- Effects of muscle disuse: muscles that are not used consistently will shorten, impacting joints and may eventually require surgery. Individuals need to be kept active throughout the day.

Additionally, individuals with cerebral palsy often have associated sensory, cognition, communication, medical and social issues that need to be considered when designing an AAC system and determining access. Individuals with cerebral palsy may have atypical feedback from skin, muscles, and joints. They may dislike being helped with motor movements. Because the body does not receive accurate information, the individual may make inappropriate responses.

There may be issues with balance, with vision, and with hearing. Vision issues impact use of picture-based communication. Vestibular system disorders may cause the individual to have either no fear of falling or abnormally strong fear. There may be a strong need to move; to bang feet, jump or rock. Once engaged in such movement they may have difficulty controlling themselves.

Individuals with cerebral palsy may have difficulty with attention, memory, cognition (which is impossible to determine without communication). There are a variety of medical issues associated with cerebral palsy that can impact communication skills and access to AAC. Positioning is not just important for access to the AAC system, but the impact of poor positioning can negatively affect internal organs or muscles and joints, and increase interference with access.

In using an AAC system, individuals may have difficulty with reaching, pointing, looking at, waving. Those behaviors may be inconsistent. Assessors may have difficulty identifying if the individual is being intentional. Looking at the communication system while reaching for it may be difficult and inconsistent.

The overflow of movement can impact the communication partner's interpretation of their response. Individuals with cerebral palsy experience significant dyspraxia - difficulty with planning and executing motor movements - as they attempt to control and organize body movements without consistent success. A single signaling gesture may need to be specifically taught to the individual to use to communicate to a partner who understands (a "smart partner.") Ability to look at the communication display and/or the partner while making a response with the hands may continue to be inconsistent and difficult.

In assessing an individual with cerebral palsy, it is important to gather information about how he processes sensory input (from all senses) across environments and times, whether and how his responses are impacted by different sensory input, and whether response varies with type and/or intensity of various input. Does it take more or less input to generate a response? Does the individual have strong defensive responses to input? How long does it take to establish attention and how long can it be maintained? How well can the individual see and hear? Cortical vision impairment (CVI) - involving damage to area(s) of the brain responsible for processing visual input - is often found in individuals with cerebral palsy. (CVI is explained in more detail below). What type of consistent response can be established for the individual to use yes and no or modified pointing responses with partner assisted scanning? What type of response can be used to activate a switch or joystick or head mouse to access a high-tech device? What movement pattern(s) can be established for a "yes" and "No" response?

In teaching AAC to an individual with such significant motor issues, we are, in fact, often attempting to teach him to learn to do two difficult things simultaneously. Erickson has developed a plan for integrating academic, communication and motor programs for students with significant disabilities. She suggests identifying activities based on a color-coded system where

<u>Red</u> represents

1. an activity that is cognitively and linguistically challenging

2. communication that includes new vocabulary or symbols or access system

3. motor positions or requirements that require work to maintain head and trunk control, whose physical demands interfere with the ability to communicate and/or participate

Yellow represents

4. an activity that is moderately challenging or review of material at the instructional level

5. communication whose symbols or vocabulary have been introduced and used

6. motor position where the child is not completely supported but can be maintained with effort, where the position does not completely interfere with the ability to participate

Green represents

7. an activity at the child's independent level; limited cognitive challenge

8. communication system that can be used with good success

9. position that is fully supported and access is maximized; minimal physical effort needed to sustain position

Erickson suggests pairing a red cognitive task with green communication systems and positions; yellow cognitive and linguistic tasks with yellow or green communication systems and positions; green cognitive and linguistic tasks with red or yellow communication systems and positions.

This paradigm is crucial when developing an AAC system for an individual with cerebral palsy or other motor impairment and considering access. Remembering that AAC is a system of components will help with thinking about multiple modes of access that fit the red, yellow, and green parameters, and matching them to complementary modes of communication.

In intervention, it will be particularly important to think about which parts or components of the communication system are used when accessing familiar vocabulary versus new vocabulary, so that difficult modes of access are not used when learning new vocabulary in difficult activities but can be in use when communicating in familiar and independent activities with known vocabulary.

Rett Syndrome:

Rett syndrome is largely a disorder of apraxia - the inability to perform purposeful motor movements; to reliably connect an action to the thought of acting (Burkhart). As the syndrome progresses, the child loses purposeful use of her hands and the ability to speak. Other early symptoms may include problems crawling or walking and decreased eye contact. The loss of functional use of the hands is followed by compulsive hand movements such as wringing and washing. These movements are not intentional and often uncontrollable. They may increase with fatigue and stress, anxiety, or pain. In order to establish reliable movements for accessing an AAC system, these movements must be overridden.

Working with an individual with Rett syndrome requires patience. When looking for a response, wait time must be provided. Continued asking or prompting will actually elongate the period of waiting. The system is working to try to initiate an action. Providing the initial stimulus again merely reboots the system and makes it start over again. Remember, the harder she tries, the harder it becomes to respond.

Because eye movements are also impacted, the individual may look away from the partner or task, seeming to be uninterested, when, in fact, the movement is uncontrolled. Because these girls have difficulty with using eye gaze and gestures consistently it is often assumed they aren't able to communicate or have sufficient cognitive skills for some activities.

Individuals with Rett often use proxemics - closeness or proximity to the communication partner - and body movements to communicate. They may lean on or toward a desired item or person, they may vocalize, laugh or cry. These behaviors may appear to be nonlinguistic, however, if responded to and acknowledged as communicative by a partner, they can be shaped into more meaningful responses.

These girls can learn (girls have an overwhelming majority over boys). And most maintain active interest in socialization. Establishing a consistent yes/no response is a good place to start. Asking yes/no questions does not usually require a picture communication system; simply the partner's participation and understanding of the individual's responses. Burkhart (2014) recommends using switches if needed to establish head movements. Placement of voice output switches near the individual's head that activate when the head movement is made (without necessarily needing to hit them) provides auditory feedback to establish the pattern. If needed, do have the user actually use the switches to also provide tactile feedback. Fade the switches so that yes and no responses can be made independent of them.

Eye gaze can be a strength for some girls with Rett, despite the pattern of eye movements, but may alternately be difficult for others. Newer eye gaze technology allows for better "reading" of the eyes despite these movements. Girls with Rett syndrome are often able to learn to use eye gaze as a communication access mode, either with high-technology systems or with paper-based eye gaze books. Systems employing partner assisted scanning are also used. High-tech eye gaze can allow for more independent communication for Rett girls. Choosing an eye gaze system that allows for extraneous head and eye movements is important. An extended trial period is always recommended; especially because the high-tech systems differ greatly from one to the other.

A supplemental component to the system is also required when utilizing eye gaze, due to fatigue of eye muscles and intermittent difficulty with controlling the gaze. Using a partner assisted scanning system is recommended. Sometimes pointing is not enough to focus the individual's attention on the picture symbol. A pick-up-and-show system might be used. Two copies of each communication book page are created and laminated. One set is cut into individual symbols, which are Velcro'd into their correct locations in the book. The communication partner picks up and shows the symbols while verbally scanning them, so that the girl can focus her attention and make a correct selection.

Bartolotta suggests the following Best Practices in AAC intervention for Rett individuals:

- Begin by teaching a simple requesting response

- Ensure the targeted response is within the individual's physical abilities – consider nonstandard behaviors

- Consider a simple motor act rather than speech or gestures (touch a switch, use a hand movement or natural gesture)

- Assess use of eye gaze

- Offer choices

- Develop consistency across two favored objects

- Explore expanding set to three or more choices

- Begin with no-tech; establish a consistent, valid level of response while allowing time to respond (many individuals with Rett have delayed responses)

Cortical Vision Impairment:

Vision, more than any other system, allows the individual to take in massive amounts of stimuli from the environment for the brain to act upon. In the process, the individual gazes at things, does so in specific sequences, focuses on specific details in order for the brain to make decisions about what to do.

Vision develops as a process of neurological development and maturation. Our ability to process visual stimuli and attach meaning to them - called "seeing" - involves not only a healthy vision system, but also healthy neurological system. When a child is born with a neurological disorder, it is likely that a visual impairment will exist. Development of the visual system through learning through interaction with the environment is also impaired when a child has motor impairment. Eyes do not tell the individual what to do. The brain's experiences do. Without these experiences, or when the experiences are impaired in some way, the brain cannot tell the individual how to act and react.

"The current leading cause of visual impairment among children is not a disease or condition of the eyes, but Cortical Vision Impairment (CVI) - also known as cerebral visual impairment - in which visual dysfunction is caused by damage or injury to the brain." (American Printing House)

There is a differentiation between ocular disorders where the pathology of the eyes is directly impacted, and neurological disorders where there is impaired or reduced vision due to an impairment or injury to the brain. Cortical vision impairment is not related to visual acuity; it occurs due to brain damage. CVI is a neurological visual disorder. It results in unique visual responses to objects and people in the environment. An eye exam usually yields normal results, but there is a history of neurological issues and the presence of defining characteristics of CVI (below). CVI may be seen in individuals who have suffered asphyxia, traumatic brain injury, infection of the brain or brain maldevelopment. The student's medical history will include neurological problems rather than problems with the ocular system. The individual may be non-responsive visually and responsiveness will be inconsistent, but this is not due to a problem with the eyes.

Cortical vision impairment is the most common cause of vision impairment in children in the U.S. It is seen in children who are premature, who have a neurological disorder, or have had acquired brain injury. Given that 40%-80% of the brain is required to process vision, brain damage in almost any area can lead to CVI. The brain loses its ability to integrate and organize visual input received from the eyes.

Shaman (2009) offers this example of typical people trying to understand what CVI feels like: Imagine that you are looking at a blackboard full of complicated math equations, much higher than your level of math. You can see all the numbers and symbols, but you cannot understand what you are seeing. Similarly, a child with CVI may see a world full of colors and shapes with perfect acuity, but he may not have any idea what he is seeing. The child may not make meaning from the visual images and may not know that the colors and shapes are a car, a hat, or his mother.

According to Roman-Lantzy, who has written the definitive book on CVI, in infants the vision will change in either direction; better or worse, but won't remain static. Cortical vision impairment responds to rehabilitation in infancy during the period of plasticity. If there is good environmental support and stability of the neurological system, then progress will be permanent.

In older students, progress may be slower; however, since the end of the period of plasticity is unknown, rehabilitation should continue. Intervention should be integrated into daily activities, not just be a separate time of isolated vision stimulation.

Roman Lantzy tells us students with CVI show:

- distinct color preferences - most often bright red or yellow, but may also be any color that is familiar to the child. Individuals with CVI might see colors without being able to identify them. During activities, create a "negative" or neutral background by placing items on a black or grey background; especially communication systems with complex displays. Communication symbols should have red or yellow (or other preferred color as per assessment) backgrounds, or have red or yellow outlines and text on black backgrounds. Intervention may need to start by presenting preferred color objects. Individuals with CVI will often respond better to color than to black and white symbols.

- attraction to movement - a need for movement to elicit or sustain visual attention. The area of the brain that processes visual movement is deeper in the brain than the visual cortex, so is often unaffected. It is easier for the individual to see movement than isolated objects. Shake objects or pictures to gain attention. Shake a flashlight around on the picture to focus attention. Place a preferred color film over the flashlight to create a colored light and move the light over the item to be focused on. Broken balloons also work well for creating a colored light. Use objects with shiny or reflective surfaces (a pinwheel, Mylar pom-pom). Sometimes the child can see better when he is moving; such as in a rocking chair or when driving a power wheelchair.

- visual latency - a delayed response in looking at objects. Wait for a response and notice the conditions under which a lag occurs. Latency can vary on context.

- visual field preferences - the presence of unusual field locations in addition to loss of visual field. Present moving objects in the right, left, upper, and/or lower peripheral fields. Note which way the student turns his head to look at items. Sometimes the visual field loss is in the center. The differences in the student's visual field can change over time, as visual attention is practiced.

- difficulties with visual and environmental complexity - the student has difficulty when the object itself is a complex display, or the object is seen in an environment that is a complex display, or the item is being viewed at the same time as there are other stimuli competing for attention. Visual fields appear crowded. Try presenting objects in the student's preferred color, then two and then three colors, then in a pattern.

- light gazing or visual stare - the individual might stare at a light source

- absent or atypical visual reflex responses - the reflex to blink in response to an approaching object is impaired.

- difficulties with visual novelty - prefers viewing familiar objects, lacks curiosity to view novel items. Symbols in the AAC system need to maintain stability for the brain to develop pathways.

- <u>absence of visually guided reach</u> - the ability to look at and touch something at the same time is absent, and the two actions are performed separately. It is difficult for the individual to attend to looking at something and reaching for it simultaneously. The two actions require significant concentration and cognitive energy. Consider Erickson's Red-Yellow-Green Light analogy discussed above. Again, stability of location of items is important. Look for differences if the background is plain vs complex.

- <u>difficulty with distance viewing</u> - the child may only attend in near-space. This happens because the child is trying to suppress background information. Items at a distance become part of the larger, confusing background.

Any or all of these characteristics or visual behaviors lead to children being unable to use their vision in the usual way. These students may not look at or pay attention visually to things we expect them to. They may fix their attention on unusual items; such as moving ceiling fan blades.

In addition, the child with CVI may have difficulty with contrast, which impacts ability to read facial expressions; with multiple sensory input, which impacts ability to use vision and listening at the same time; with depth perception; with recognizing spatial relationships of objects in the room; with visually recognizing objects or persons. Individuals with CVI have impaired social skills. They cannot read facial expressions and others may believe they are refusing to look at persons or objects. And, as a result, they have difficulty with interpersonal communication.

The individual's vision may appear to change from moment to moment. This is not actually happening. It is the changes in the environment that impact the individual's ability to see a specific stimulus. This can require that the communication system be moved frequently. Communication partners need to constantly be assessing the location or position of the display when there are changes in the environment.

Improvement is both likely and possible with training. This requires discovering the CVI at an early age and providing direct intervention. (Roman-Lantzy, C., 2007) Children with CVI have the capacity to see more effectively and can learn effectively given an adequate plan and intervention.

From both neurological and education perspectives, brain plasticity is the mechanism for improved vision. Visual function improves by: high frequency, repetitive, and consistent visual and visual- motor experiences embedded in familiar and meaningful routines and carefully designed to meet the unique needs of each child. (Edelman, et al., 2006; Roman-Lantzy, 2007)

There are 2 types of cortical vision impairment. Lower Level CVI involves damage of the visual pathway up to and including the striate cortex, affecting the child's acuity, understanding of visual images, and ability to see parts of visual fields. The child may only notice specific objects.

Higher Level CVI, sometimes referred to as cognitive visual impairment, involves damage occurring beyond the striate cortex and disrupts specific vision functions (such as awareness of movement, shape, or color) but does not involve visual field or visual acuity. (Shaman 2009)

This distinction is important in understanding how the individual with CVI is seeing the visual field. Seeing involves taking in the visual scene, finding and recognizing parts of that visual scene, deciding what to focus on, and engaging in visually directed movement. Our brain subconsciously decides what information is relevant and what is not. When areas of the brain decide, together, to select relevant information the individual attends to it. This visual attention is often damaged in individuals with CVI.

In symbol-based communication systems consider the color, size, and background of pictures, the visual complexity of the system and the child's visual field preferences. Use preferred colors in symbol backgrounds, or highlight the symbol outline and text in preferred color on a black or grey background. Control the amount or complexity of information presented visually; reduce how much information is on a page.

Simplifying the visual environment is crucial at all stages of developing a visual array. Line drawings are actually better than photos. Provide movement to focus the individual's attention on the communication display. Use shiny, reflective surfaces for gaining attention by surrounding or wrapping items in Mylar or a similar material. However, when laminating pages, use anti-glare, or matter, laminate. Put the communication device or book on a black background by laying a black paper or cloth over the desk or stand. (fig 1)

In general, individuals with CVI experience success with AAC systems that utilize partner assisted scanning, tactile systems with voice output, auditory scanning high-tech voice output devices, two-switch auditory step scanning where the user can control the speed of scanning for processing, that utilize visual tracking of a visual stimulus across the scan (such as a flashlight or finger or bright object). Burkhart also suggests "using a communication device (BIGmack Communicator) using color coding. For example, pair a 2-D picture with a similar 3-D object using bright colors. Have the communicator in the same color (i.e. Have a picture of a red cup, have a red cup and a red communicator that says, "I want a drink," when accessed."

Additional tips for AAC use with these students:

- Use Partner Assisted Scanning or use devices with auditory scanning. These modes of access allow for success by removing the need to visually attend to and shift from pictures the students can't see; there is now no need for communication success to be dependent upon symbol recognition.

- Abandon the kind of standard objectives you set for other AAC users. These students will have difficulty or lack of success with objectives to match objects to pictures, make requests using picture boards a specified number of times, or identify named pictures in arrays. Matching and identification tasks are largely nonfunctional, anyway.

- Avoid vocabulary that only relates to a single activity and then doesn't get used again; use of core vocabulary or high frequency vocabulary is beneficial for those individuals.
- Avoid limited choices that don't allow engagement. This is true for many students. Multiple choice responses do not encourage language development or elaborate interactions.

Provide social contact vocabulary so that the individual can maintain social interaction and engagement with others, even when unable to see what is going on.

Provide vocabulary that is stable and can be added to as skills develop. This, again, encourages the use of core vocabulary, where words have multiple meaning uses with a limited number of visual distinctions.

Provide vocabulary sets that are organized and stay the same each time. Stability of vocabulary becomes even more critical for users who cannot see the displays. In partner assisted scanning it becomes important for the vocabulary to come in the same order each time. Individuals learn to anticipate where vocabulary comes in the list, so as to make themselves ready to respond.

Make changes slowly

Use consistent language for tasks, questions, etc.

Incorporate function into all activity; look careful at classroom tasks to make sure that they have a functional purpose for the individual. Don't make intervention for vision independent of functional activities and contextual routines.

Similarly, keep communication intervention grounded in function.

Make sure conversational or other communication interactions are important to the individual. Don't just talk to practice a specific skill or to address the classroom curriculum. While the child's participation may initially be limited to vocalizations, eye gaze or facial expressions, keeping his attention keeps him involved in learning. Expand the conversation to build the child's sense of anticipation, turn taking, and interacting. Add to the interaction one piece at a time, build up the constancy and routine, then expand again. (S 2009) suggests that partners use differently colored and textured gloves during interactions to build visual interest and routine.

Integrate movement into activities to capture and maintain attention. Pay attention to what captures the child's attention and use it or incorporate it in other interactions and routines. Mylar often works well with children with CVI because it both moves and reflects. Maintain specific colors into matching routines consistently. The child can begin to associate color to function, for example plates can always be red, cups can always be blue, in all environments. (see Burkhart's suggestion above)

Build repetition, constancy and routine into activities for learning communication. Again, routines serve as a stepping stone to building language. Consistency in colors, background, items used, location of activities all build routine and patterns.

Build in socialization. Individuals with CVI have limited opportunities to play and socialize. Girls with Rett, in particular, are very social and enjoy being with others and interacting in any way possible. Engineer the play so that the child with CVI can participate. That may be just to laugh, or it can involve using a switch to communicate something. Keep the individual actively participating. Create a familiar routine out of the play, with a consistent beginning and end, so that the child learns the routine and, eventually, the language that goes with it.

Consider building touch into the system. Most children with CVI can learn from touch and will probably have strong likes and dislikes. Consider the deepness of pressure, speed, pattern and location of the touch. Build touch into routines as a cue to help define parts of the routine, or the beginning and end. Building texture into the visual system may also be beneficial.

Down Syndrome:

Down Syndrome is not always regarded as a special population that requires AAC intervention. Many individuals with Down syndrome develop verbal skills to varying degrees. However, sometimes their verbal skills are not sufficient to meet all communication needs, and, even more often, their speech is highly unintelligible, even after receiving speech therapy as children.

Research suggests that as many as 95% of parents often have difficulty understanding their child's speech. Speech disorders with Down syndrome are usually related to oral motor weakness or anatomical differences. Specifically, problems include:

Central nervous system structures that are atypical and result in difficulties with timing, accuracy, and sequencing of speech movements

Large tongue size, that is larger than appropriate relative to oral cavity size, that impacts tongue placement for articulation.

Abnormal development of facial bones and relatively smaller skull size may result in a smaller oral cavity, with the same impact.

Differentiation of the mid facial muscles may be impacted, with a resulting impact on facial expression and oral movement.

Hypotonia may cause a variety of difficulties with muscle coordination and movement. Speech requires the coordination of a large number of muscles for respiration, phonation, resonation and articulation, and hypotonia results in poor intelligibility. Both articulation and vocal quality can be affected.

Additionally, disorders of fluency affect between 45% - 55% of individuals with Down syndrome. Dysfluencies tend to increase with those individuals with better expressive language.

AAC interventions with Down syndrome do not generally impact speech production. However, for those individuals with Down syndrome who do not have effective expressive communication it is important to introduce AAC at a young enough age to avoid development of frustration and avoidance behaviors, and to develop effective repair strategies.

CAS (Childhood Apraxia of Speech):

Developmental Apraxia of Speech (DAS), also called Childhood Apraxia of Speech (CAS) has historically been a controversial area of speech disorders. There has been significant debate over whether the disorder exists, whether it should rightfully be called Dyspraxia (rather than Apraxia) and whether or how to remediate it. Definitions can differ, but include the central area of difficulty - the inability to or difficulty with production of volitional movements required for speech, in the absence of weakness or paralysis of muscles used in speech production.

Unlike other disorders, children with DAS usually appear to develop typically, only excepting the area of speech production. Children with this disorder may be sensitive to textures of certain food, may dislike having their teeth brushed. There may be some other "soft" neurological signs, including overall clumsiness.

AAC intervention is sometimes resisted because these children have no obvious sign of disability. Parents often wish to wait and work on speech production. They may not want to "create" to look of a disability by providing an external speech device.

The motor planning deficits of DAS impact articulation and prosody of speech. Intelligibility of speech and functional use of communication may be severely reduced. The articulation skills of these children often show:

Reduced consonant and vowel production

Error patterns of omission and cluster reduction and assimilation predominate

Vowels are especially disordered in production

Articulation errors may not be consistent

Children with DAS often use the simplest syllable sounds they are able, and intelligibility decreases as length of speech production increases; children may be relatively intelligible at the 1-2 syllable level, but intelligibility disappears in connected speech

Groping behaviors are apparent in speech of these children

The impact of AAC intervention on speech production is not consistent, but the ability to effectively communicate has a tremendous impact.

ASD (Autism Spectrum Disorder):

Students with autism spectrum disorder (ASD) face a variety of challenges: including communication impairment (which leads often to behavior challenges), sensory processing challenges, and social interaction challenges.

Impairments in verbal and nonverbal communication are core features of children on the Autism Spectrum. Individuals with autism often fail to use communication for social purposes, to use standard communication gestures or expressions, or to process many of the auditory-verbal signals used in communication.

Individuals with autism may have difficulty with understanding why we communicate, what mode to use to communicate, and when and where to communicate effectively with others. Individuals with ASD use many behaviors to communicate, but also those that are not communicative. What often differentiates them is how their communication partners react and respond to them. Additionally, individuals with ASD do not always understand why to use appropriate communication modes. They may use some behaviors to communicate the messages that are most important to them, and not yet see the other reasons to communicate, which are often more socially directed or related. Individuals with ASD may not be aware that they need to get the attention of a partner before they can communicate; that when and where are dependent upon the context, particularly a context which involves another person.

Early and consistent intervention with AAC has been correlated with increased communication - both aided and verbal - in individuals with ASD. The strength in visual processing is positive for use of visual AAC strategies. Difficulty with motor movements are aided by use of an expressive mode that requires less motor involvement. And the high level of interest in technology and interactive objects found in individuals with autism makes a visual and technological solution a good fit for these individuals.

Use of picture augmented input and visual cues has consistently been found to be evidence-based practice for students with ASD. Visual supports may help individuals with ASD to compensate for inattention, and with auditory processing, sequencing, and organizing information. Use of picture communication systems and voice output devices also listed as evidence-based practice by the National Professional Development Center on Autism Spectrum Disorders. http://autismpdc.fpg.unc.edu/content/briefs

Use of PODD (Pragmatic Organized Dynamic Display) style of communication books has shown great promise with many individuals with Autism Spectrum Disorder.

The Evidence-Based Practice and Autism in the Schools guide published by the collaboration of the National Autism Center/National Standards Project lists the following:

Established AAC treatments:

- Schedules, including visual strategies to communicate a series of activities or steps for a specific activity

- Story-based intervention package, including written stories depicting specific situations or events, describing expected behaviors

Emerging AAC treatments

- AAC devices, including interventions with high-tech and low-tech strategies; such as pictures, photos or symbols to facilitate communication development

- PECS, a specific AAC strategy based on applied behavior analysis principles

- Sign instruction

- Direct instruction of signs to improve functional communication

Unestablished treatment

- Facilitated Communication, providing physical support to assist an individual to point to pictures, word, letters

The National Professional Development Center on Autism Spectrum Disorders found six evidence-based practices related to AAC:

Speech generating devices/voice output devices - low and high-tech devices

Functional communication training - use of AAC strategies and tools to replace unexpected forms of communication

PECS

Social narratives where social situations are described, with behavioral expectations and/or routines embedded within a story using visual cues

Video modeling using video recording and display to model target behaviors

Visual supports, using visual tools to assist students in transitioning to and completing activities throughout the day

There is overlap between the two groups of findings (Corporale, 2013), and readers should note that the NAC/NSP reviews focused on evidence to support improvement of verbal communication (using SGD and PECS) while the NPDC focused on increased expressive communication and language using SGDs and functional communication using PECS.

Additionally, there were identified important factors for successful implementation of AAC: use of motivating vocabulary, correct symbol and array sizes, encouraging communication throughout multiple appropriate opportunities, and training of communication partners.

Reviews of literature since the publication of those findings have identified common best practice strategies to include:

Use of multimodal approach

Close collaboration among staff

Staff and peer training

AAC implementation that includes relevant, meaningful activities

Providing functional communication strategies across environments

Involving the family in the AAC assessment and implementation process

Involvement of the SLP in a primary role, with involvement of all other communication partners

Consultative role of SLP is supported by other partners

It is obvious that these practices extend beyond use with individuals with ASD, across all populations learning to use AAC.

Embedding communication into routines helps students with ASD learn to communicate within those routines, just as it does with all AAC and language learners. Pre-symbolic students can use objects during natural routines, to build language skills. Students can learn in natural contexts with natural objects to initiate communication. Use of object boards for choice making or insertion of communication into routines with associated objects fosters language and communication development.

Emergent communicators with ASD do well with choice making with visual supports of AAC. Symbols can be inserted into routines to show the steps of a task or activity. Use of gestures can be inserted into routines to signal intents or feelings to partners. Use of just the word, "No," for early communicators can provide an outlet for the frustrations of not being able to deal with the environment and its demands.

Above all, use of aided input strategies not only provides models for expressive communication with pictures, but a bridge to comprehension of language by individuals with ASD. Individuals who do not comprehend the language used by others or those who can comprehend, but have it leave their memory so quickly that they may as well not have understood, live life in a heightened state of anxiety. Not understanding what has been said to you, what is going to happen next, what you need to do first, how the routine for the day is being changed, how much work you need to do, when the task will be over must be amazingly baffling.

Many individuals with ASD develop their own set of coping behaviors and routines. For them things need to be done the same way all of the time, arranged in the same way, or maintained in status quo to help them deal with an unpredictable and unintelligible world. They might perseverate on a behavior or phrase. They insist on sameness, because they do not understand the language others use to explain changes. For these individuals using aided picture communication provides communication comprehension, as well as a model for expression. Use of pictures that are not as transient as speech, that are stable and permanent provides more sense of stability and understanding. Communication must be understood before it can be used.

Drager (2009) reviewed the literature on use of Aided Language Input with individuals with ASD. The variety of aided input strategies have the following features in common:

> They are implemented in naturally occurring opportunities, with all communication partners.
>
> They augment the input the individual receives.
>
> They use modeling to expand vocabulary.
>
> The intervention takes place in naturally occurring contexts and is embedded into functional and meaningful activities.

Because children with ASD have strengths in visual-spatial skills, use of Aided Language Stimulation should not only be effective in providing AAC modeling but also for supporting comprehension of verbal input. Research results available to date, while limited, indicate that providing Aided Input, through a variety of specific strategies all increase the comprehension and use of children with ASD studied.

Limiting the use of navigation through use of core vocabulary displays is useful for many users with ASD who do not consistently attend to navigation paths and who impulsively hit buttons without intent.

Because social roles and demands are integral to communication, social skills through communication need to be taught to individuals with autism spectrum disorder. The following social goals are recommended by the Ohio Dept. of Education:

- Imitation and joint attention (attending with others)
- Understanding personal space
- Acceptable environmental behaviors, such as not picking nose in public, bathroom etiquette, etc.
- Emotions of self and others

- Identification of emotions and where they occur

- How individual actions affect others

- Asking for help/assistance

- Slang, sarcasm, joking, teasing

- Initiating, maintaining and reciprocating social interactions

- Accepting rejection by peers

- Playing games, winning and losing graciously

- Turn-taking, waiting for turn

- The meaning of body language (includes facial and bodily gestures)

- Age appropriate behavior with the opposite sex, e.g., recognizing unwanted sexual advances and dealing with them appropriately, understanding appropriate sexual expression and seeking privacy for any sexual expression, finding appropriate ways of seeking and giving affection

- Typical peers' understanding and successful ways to interact and support the individual with ASD/PDD

- Appropriate workplace behavior as a part of the transition from school to work. This includes the use of vocational language, how to take work breaks, dealing with the public, and working with superiors, subordinates and work peers. In many cases, the degree to which a person with ASD/PDD "fits in" with, and is accepted by, their work peers will determine their long-term job success. The employer may require assistance with appropriately introducing the person with ASD to the workplace and educating the workers with how to have a meaningful work relation with that person. On the other hand, once acceptance is gained from work peers, the person with ASD often has a very strong, vocal support network that greatly enhances the probability of their long-term job retention and success.

In addition to providing AAC intervention the following communication intervention strategies are recommended for individuals with ASD (Ohio Dept. Health):

- Decrease asking questions and increase use of comments and descriptions of activities, emotions, and environments that the individual experiences.

  - The communicating partner needs to fully understand that situations, certain individuals, sensory issues and stress will affect the quality of communication and the communication intention.

  - Modify the speaker's language and provide visual supports

  - Allow time for auditory processing and formulation of information.

  - Develop a protocol to gain the individual's attention. The protocol should include how to initiate joint focused attention.

  - Encourage meaningful imitation. Since imitation is one of the precursors to the development of functional language, build in ample opportunities for activities to develop imitative skills.

  - Help the individual focus attention on the speaker. This will maximize the impact of any direction, question, or information.

  - Determine the communicative intent and other possible functions of non-verbal and verbal behaviors to establish their meaning.
  - Integrate communication strategies into all daily activities. Teach communication strategies in a step-by-step approach, starting in an organized environment, and integrating into all environments.

- Use vocabulary and grammatical structure at the individual's comprehension level.

- Consider using rhythm and music.

- Teach turn-taking and joint attention.

- Provide the individual with multiple opportunities to initiate interactions, make choices, and have peer-to-peer contact on a daily basis across all environments.

- Support receptive communication as well as expressive communication through both nonverbal and verbal methods: visual supports (object boards, pictures, gestures, sign language) and voice output communication devices.

- Facilitate the initiation of conversation and provide opportunities to practice language rather than waiting for the individual to initiate contact.

- During transitions from classes, buildings, work: offer a summary of successful communication strategies to appropriate personnel.

Alternate Access

1. Pick up and Give or Show (Burkhart 2016) involves the symbols being Velcro'd to the book pages. It is important to note that this involves Velcro-ing the same symbol to its exact spot on the page; matching it to the symbol on the page. This is not a system where you can return symbols anywhere on the page. A second copy of the page is laminated, cut apart, and used for the images that are grasped. This is useful for individuals who do not have the ability to or do not understand the concept of a point, but can grasp and hold out the symbol.

   The symbols are placed on a strip to construct a message of sequenced symbols for those individuals who can sequence symbols into phrases or sentences. Seeing the entire message aids with memory and formulation. This method can also be used with individuals with limited comprehension who have difficulty with visual tracking, as a way to provide aided input.

Limitations to this method of access include a significantly heavier and expanded book, due to the multiple layers of each page; the need for extra time to grasp and hold out the symbols; the need for fine motor skills to grab and hold the symbol(s); the additional time needed to replace the symbols in the book when the message is completed; the possible distraction from the engagement of the interaction caused by the physical activity of this method. Communication partners may limit the exchange due to the time and physical necessities. Conversational interactions may be cut short due to time constraints.

2. Partner-Assisted Scanning involves the communication partner providing scanning of the symbols by showing/pointing to and/or verbally naming the items in a low-tech book or board. The individual must be able to respond with a yes or no gesture of some sort with some reliability and consistency.

Partner Assisted Scanning (PAS) can be visual, auditory, or both. In visual scanning the individual uses visual recognition of the symbols. The partner scans through the choices with a finger, pointer, or light, without verbal input. In auditory scanning the partner reads the names of the symbols. The individual must recognize the spoken names. The partner needs to read the names, NOT ask questions; such as, "Do you feel sick?"

Auditory and visual scanning combines the two approaches. The partner both shows and reads the labels for each symbol. This method helps individuals who know the spoken names but are just learning to recognize the symbols. This is also useful for individuals with CVI who rely on the auditory input but can use the visual input to improve visual skills.

The AAC learner can use a single movement/gesture to accept (say, "Yes") when the correct item or row or column is spoken/shown. This is how individuals using switches and scanning usually respond with high-tech devices. Partners need to be aware of the response lag/wait time for the individual.

The AAC learner can also use two movements to accept and/or reject items as scanned. The child needs to make two differentiated responses to say "yes" or "No" to each item or row or column as it is scanned. This is less taxing on the partner but more tiring for the individual.

Scanning of symbols on the board/page can be linear, where each item is scanned in a row one at a time, either left to right (one row at a time) or top to bottom (one column at a time).

Scanning can also be column/item, where the scanning starts with the first column and proceeds through each column until the user selects one. Then the scanning goes from the top of that column down, until the user accepts the desired symbol.

Scanning can also use sections of the display. Symbols are grouped together, and the user selects the group that contains the desired symbol. Then the partner scans the columns in that section, then across the row that holds the indicated symbol.

3. Coded access for eye gaze involves using colors to section the areas of the communication display. Coded access is available with the eye gaze PODD displays. There is a separate display that indicates columns by different colors and rows by different numbers. The user first indicates which section (quadrant) of the display has the desired symbol. Then the user indicates which color to tell the column, then which number to tell the row. When there is a large number of symbols on the display this significantly speeds up the rate of communication.

4. Combined access is provided in the PODD templates for individuals who use a combination of eye gaze or pointing and partner assisted scanning. Symbols are clustered together, and the individual indicates which group using eye gaze or direct selection of the area. Then the partner scans the choices. This increases the size of vocabulary available to the user on a given page or board.

5. High contrast symbols are available for some symbols in the PCS set from Mayer-Johnson. Other symbols can often be created with high contrast by altering the button's background and/or border colors.

CHAPTER 9

Getting through the IEP

T he IEP document is unique to the United States. Although other countries have special education systems and services, they differ from each other and from our system. Our system has undergone many changes since the first implementation of Public Law 94-142.

I am including this information simply as an assist to parents - and new professionals - in the IEP development.

AAC is most commonly found in the "Special Factors" section of the IEP document. This mention should include not just "an AAC system," but the specific type of system/device, the type of symbols, and the array/display specifics.

I have often been asked, "How do I include AAC goals in the IEP?" For the most part, including the AAC system in the language objectives is not necessary; the AAC system is simply the mode of response. Where this differs, however, is when there is discussion of the operational and strategic skills; these are unique to the AAC user's system and skills.

Your AAC user should have had a complete AAC evaluation in order to determine the particular system to be used. This evaluation should have included trying at least 3 different systems, with different array sizes and symbols used and, if appropriate, different selection or access modes.

I am sometimes asked if the student "really" needs an evaluation if they are already using a system that has been given to them. The answer is, "Maybe." The answer would be dependent upon what the system is, whether it has sufficiently robust vocabulary, and how well the student has been using it. If the system is meeting the student's needs and will provide sufficient vocabulary and morpho-syntactic structure into the immediate and longer-term future, we might determine that it should be continued to be used, with or without adjustments. But if the system does not meet these criteria, then it should be replaced.

While we may not necessarily have specific objectives for use of the AAC system we do want to make sure we have sufficient language objectives to continue to grow their skills. Objectives should include targets for core words, extended vocabulary, and syntax. They should also include targets for communication functions beyond requesting or labeling.

One tool available to guide the IEP is the Augmentative & Alternative Communication Profile, by Tracy Kovach. This checklist provides specific points across the 4 areas of competency delineated by Light; operational, strategic, social and linguistic Using this checklist provides clear guidance for determining objectives.

Sometimes the first objective for our students is simply to pay attention to a communication partner providing Aided Language Stimulation. Porter (2009) reminds us that many children require years of language input before developing expressive language.

Often IEP goals for AAC are written based on adults' ideas about what the student will want to say and how often he will want to say it in specific situations. Some examples given by Porter and Burkhart (2009) include objectives written to request (X) a number of times and objectives written to respond to questions.

In the first instance, we really do not know if the student will want (X) on any given day or in any given activity. If he doesn't ask for it that many times is it because he doesn't want it? Or doesn't want it that often? What does he learn about communicating if he has to ask for something he doesn't want?

In the second example, how do we "score" his responses? Does he get credit for responding to a question even if the answer is wrong?

Writing goals for a child to say something a specified number of times could teach him inappropriately and provide him with less real communicating. Porter insists that goals should be flexible enough for the child to say what he wants to, while helping him to say it more completely or correctly. Goals should never be written for the child to say what somebody else wants him to say.

Be sure to write goals that expand the number of communication functions the child can use; increasing the range of intents he uses.

REFERENCES

"AAC & Autism Report Implementing Evidence Based Practices in the Classroom." ClosingTheGap. N.p., Apr. 2013. Web. 29 Apr. 2015.

Angermeier, Katie, Ralf W. Schlosser, James K. Luiselli, Caroline Harrington, and Beth Carter. "Effects of Iconicity on Requesting with the Picture Exchange Communication System in Children with Autism Spectrum Disorder." Research in Autism Spectrum Disorders 2.3 (2008): 430-46. Elsevier. Web. 29 Apr. 2015.

Baker, B., Hill, K., Devylder, R. (2000). Core Vocabulary is the Same Across Environments, California State University at Northridge (CSUN) Conference, Los Angeles, California.

Balandin, S., & Iacono, T. (1999). A few well-chosen words. Augmentative and Alternative Communication, 14, 147–161.

Banajee, Meher, Cynthia Dicarlo, and Sarintha Buras Stricklin. "Core Vocabulary Determination for Toddlers." Augmentative and Alternative Communication 19.2 (2003): 67-73. Web.

Banajee, M., Dicarlo, C., & Stricklin, S. B. (2003). Core Vocabulary Determination for toddlers. Augmentative and Alternative Communication (AAC), 19, 67-73.

Berkowitz, S. Linguistic Skills of the Developmentally Disabled: What Are We Teaching?: ASHA Convention (November) 1988: Boston, Ma.

Beukelman, D. R. & Mirenda, P. (2005). Augmentative & Alternative Communication: Supporting Children & Adults With Complex Communication Needs. Baltimore: Paul H. Brookes Publishing Company.

Beukelman, D. R., Garrett K. L., & Yorkston, K. M. (2007). Augmentative Communication Strategies For Adults With Acute Or Chronic Medical Conditions. Baltimore: Paul H. Brookes Publishing Company.

Beukelman, D., & Mirenda, P. (1998). Augmentative and alternative communication: management of severe communication disorders in children and adults. Baltimore, MD: Paul H. Brookes Publishing Co.

Beukelman, D. R., & Mirenda, P. (2013). Augmentative and alternative communication: Supporting children and adults with complex communication needs. Baltimore, MD: Paul H. Brookes.

Binger, C. & Light, J. (2007). The effect of aided AAC modeling on the expression of multi-symbol messages by preschoolers who use AAC. Augmentative and Alternative Communication, 23, 30-43.

The Bioecological Model of Human Development. Bronfenbrenner, Urie; Morris, Pamela A. Lerner, Richard M. (Ed); Damon, William (Ed), (2006). Handbook of child psychology (6th ed.): Vol 1, Theoretical models of human development. (pp. 793-828). Hoboken, NJ, US: John Wiley & Sons Inc, 1063 pp.

Bondy, A. and Frost, L. "A Picture's Worth (A Picture's Worth: PECS and Other Visual Communication Strategies in Autism" (Topics in Autism); Woodbine House. 2002

Bonvillian, John D., Keith E. Nelson, and Jane Milnes Rhyne. "Sign Language and Autism." Journal of Autism and Developmental Disorders 11.1 (1981): 125-37. Web.

Bruno J, Trembath D. (2006) Use of aided language stimulation to improve syntactic performance during a weeklong intervention program. Augment Altern Commun. Dec;22(4):300-13.

Bruno, J. (2010). Test of aided-communication symbol performance. Pittsburgh, PA: Dynavox Meyer Johnson.

Bondy, A. and Frost, L. "A Picture's Worth (A Picture's Worth: PECS and Other Visual Communication Strategies in Autism" (Topics in Autism); Woodbine House. 2002

Burkhart, L. Rett Syndrome Assessment and Curricular Materials Modifications, ATIA; Orlando; (2014)

Burkhart, L and Porter, G. (2012) Combining Visual and Auditory Scanning for Children with CVI and Complex Communication Needs. ISAAC

Cafiero, J. Increasing Communication Skills in Students with Autism Spectrum Disorders: The AAC Technology Solutions. 1998

Calculator, S. "Use of Enhanced Natural Gestures to Foster Interactions Between Children With Angelman Syndrome and Their Parents" American Journal of Speech-Language Pathology. Vol. 11: November 2002; 340-355

Cannon, B & Edmond, G. A Few Good Words: Using Core Vocabulary to Support Nonverbal Students. The ASHA Leader. April 2009

Caporale, Betsy. A. (2013). AAC and autism report: Implementing evidence-based strategies in the classroom. Closing the Gap Solutions. Retrieved from https://www.closingthegap.com/solutions/articles/1957.

Cole, Horvath, Chapman, Deschenes, Ebeling, Sprague (2000) Adapting Curriculum and Instruction in Inclusive Classrooms

Cross, R.T., Baker, B.R., Klotz, L.S. and Badman, A.L. (1997). Static and Dynamic Keyboards: Semantic Compaction in Both Worlds. Proceedings of the 18th Annual Southeast Augmentative Communication Conference, 9-17. Birmingham: SEAC Publications

Dietz, A., Quach, W., Lund, S. K., & McKelvey, M. (2012). AAC assessment and clinical-decision making: The impact of experience. Augmentative and Alternative Communication, 28(3), 148–159. doi:10.3109/07434618.2012.704521

Drager, K. (2009). Aided modeling interventions for children with autism spectrum disorders who require AAC. Perspectives on Augmentative and Alternative Communication December 2009 vol. 18 no. 4 114-120

Erickson, K., (2003, June 24). Reading comprehension in AAC, The ASHA Leader.

Erickson, K. Integrating Academic Communication, and Motor Programs for Students with Significant Disabilities. Center for Literacy & Disabilities Studies, UNC-Chapel Hill

Erickson,K., Musselwhite, C., Ziolkowski, R. (2002) Beginning Literacy Framework. Don Johnston Inc.

Garrett, K. & Lasker, J. (2005). AAC Aphasia Categories of Communicators Checklist

Goosens, C., Crain, S., & Elder, P. (1992). Engineering the preschool environment of interactive, symbolic communication. Southeast Augmentative Communication Conference Publications. Birmingham, AL.

Gosnell, J., Costello, J., & Shane, H. (2011). A clinical approach to answer "What communication apps should we use? Perspectives on Augmentative and Alternative Communication, 20 (3), 87-96.

Hart, B. and Risely, T. (1995) Meaningful Differences in the Everyday Experience of Young American Children. Brookes Publishing, 1995

Henneberry, Solana, Jennifer Kelso, and Gloria Soto. "Using Standards-Based Instruction to Teach Language to Children Who Use AAC." ASHA, Perspectives.Web. Johnston, S., Reichle, J., Evans,J. (2004). Supporting Augmentative and Alternative Communication Use by Beginning Communicators with Severe Disabilities. American Journal of Speech-Language Pathology, 13, 20-30.

Hill, K., & Corsi, V. (2012). Role of the Speech-Language Pathologist in Assistive Technology Assessments. In S. Federici, M. J. Scherer, S. Federici, & M. J. Scherer (Eds.), Assistive Technology Assessment Handbook (pp. 301–327). Boca Raton, FL: CRC Press.

Hogdon, L. Visual Strategies for Improving Communication (Revised & Updated Edition): Practical Supports for Autism Spectrum Disorders; Quirk Roberts Publishing. 1994, 2011

Kaderavek, Joan N., and Paula Rabidoux. "Interactive To Independent Literacy: A Model For Designing Literacy Goals For Children With Atypical Communication." Reading & Writing Quarterly 20.3 (2004): 237-60. Web.

Kangas, K.A., & Lloyd, L.L. (1988). Early cognitive prerequisites to augmentative and alternative communication use: What are we waiting for? Augmentative and Alternative Communication, 4, 211-221.

Kent-Walsh, Jennifer, Cathy Binger, and Zishan Hasham. "Effects of Parent Instruction on the Symbolic Communication of Children Using Augmentative and Alternative Communication During Storybook Reading." American Journal of Speech-Language Pathology 19 (2010): 97-107.

Kent-Walsh & Binger (2013) Fundamentals of the ImPAACT Program; Perspectives on Augmentative and Alternative Communication 22(1)

Kent-Walsh, J., & McNaughton, D. (2005). Communication partner instruction in AAC: Present practices and future directions. Augmentative and Alternative Communication, 21, 195-204.

Kluth, P. Just Give Him the Whale

Korston, J. (2011) http://www.everymovecounts.net/

Light, J. (1989). Toward a definition of communicative competence for individuals using augmentative and alternative communication systems. AAC. Vol. 5, No. 2, Pages 137-144

Light, Janice. "FAQ about the Curriculum.": Literacy Instruction for Individuals with Autism, Cerebral Palsy, Down Syndrome, and Other Disabilities. Penn State University, n.d. Web. 29 Apr. 2015. <http://aacliteracy.psu.edu/index.php/page/show/id/3>.

Light, J. (1989). Towards a definition of communicative competence for individuals using augmentative and alternative communication systems. Augmentative and Alternative Communication, 5, 137-144

Light JC, Beukelman DR, Reichle J (Eds.). 2003. Communicative competence for individuals who use AAC: From research to effective practice. Baltimore: Paul H. Brookes Publishing Co.

Lonke, F. Augmentative and Alternative Communication: Models and Applications for Educators, Speech-language Pathologists Plural Publishing. 2014

Marzano, R. J. (2004). Building background knowledge for academic achievement: Research on what works in schools. Alexandria, VA: ASCD.

Mirenda, P., & Erickson, K. A. (2000). Augmentative communication and literacy. In A. M. Wetherby & B. M. Prizant (Eds.), Autism spectrum disorders: A transactional approach (pp. 333–369). Baltimore: Paul H. Brookes Publishing Co.

Mirenda,P. (2008) "A Backdoor Approach to Autism and AAC" Alternative and Augmentative Communication 24 (3), 220-234

Mirenda, P., & Iacono, T. (Eds.) (2009). Autism spectrum disorders and AAC. Baltimore: Paul H. Brookes

Musselwhite, C., & King-DeBaun, P. (1997). Emergent literacy success: Merging technology & whole language for students with disabilities. Park City, UT: Creative Communicating

National Standards Support - Addressing the Needs for Evidence Based Practice; Guidelines for ASD - National Autism Center (2009) Randolph, Ma

Nunes, Debora. "AAC INTERVENTIONS FOR AUTISM: A RESEARCH SUMMARY." INTERNATIONAL JOURNAL OF SPECIAL EDUCATION 23.2 (2008): 17-26. Web.

Ohio Department of Health, Bureau for Children with Medical Handicaps, and Bureau of Early Intervention Services. "SERVICE GUIDELINES for INDIVIDUALS with AUTISM SPECTRUM DISORDER/ PERVASIVE DEVELOPMENTAL DISORDER (ASD/PDD)." (n.d.): n. pag. Web. <http://journals.asha.org/perspectives/terms.dtl>.

Parker, Robyn. "Organizing Vocabulary for an AAC System." Kent ISD Assistive Technology /. N.p., n.d. Web. 29 Apr. 2015.

Porter, G & Kirkland, J (1995) AAC in CE integrating Augmentative and Alternative Communication into group programs: Utilising the principles of Conductive Education. Scope

Porter, G and Cafiero, J; Pragmatic Organization Dynamic Display (PODD) Communication Books: A Promising Practice for Individuals With Autism Spectrum Disorders; http://journals.asha.org/perspectives/terms.dtl>. SIG 12 Perspectives on Augmentative and Alternative Communication, December 2009, Vol. 18:121-129. doi:10.1044/aac18.4.121

Porter, G & Burkhart, L (2009) Pragmatic Organization Dynamic Display Communication Books: Designing and Implementing PODD Books. Porter and Burkhart 2009. Seminar

Predictable Chart Writing (Adapted by Hanser, 2005, from Cunningham, 2001, Hall & Williams, 2001). Compiled by The Center for Literacy and Disability Studies Department of Allied Health Sciences, University of North Carolina at Chapel Hill

Purdy, Mary, and Aimee Dietz. "Factors Influencing AAC Usage by Individuals With Aphasia." ASHA.org. N.p., Sept. 2010. Web.

Roman-Lansky, C. Cortical Visual Impairment: An Approach to Assessment and Intervention. AFB Press (August 16, 2007)

Romski MA, Sevcik RA. Breaking the speech barrier: language development through augmented means. Baltimore: Brookes, 1996.

Romski, M. A., Sevcik, R. A., Cheslock, M., & Barton, A. (2006). The System for Augmenting Language: AAC and Emerging Language Intervention. In R. McCauley & M. Fey (Eds.) Treatment of Language Disorders in Children. Baltimore: Paul H. Brookes.

Romich, B. A., Vanderheiden, G. C., & Hill, K. J. (2000). Augmentative Communication in The Biomedical Engineering Handbook second edition. Bronzino, J.D., editor. pp. 144-1 through 8. CRC Press. Boca Raton, FL.

Romski MA, Sevcik RA, Robinson BF, Mervis CB, Bertrand J. (1996) Mapping the meanings of novel visual symbols by youth with moderate or severe mental retardation. Am J Ment Retard. Jan;100(4):391-402.

Rotholz, Berkowitz, & Burberry, (1989) Functionality of two modes of communication in the community by students with developmental disabilities: A comparison of signing and communication books. Journal of the Association for Persons with Severe Handicaps, 14(3), 227 – 233.

Rowland, Charity; Schweigert, Philip. (1997) Research to Practice: Focus on: Hands-On Problem Solving Skills for Children with Deaf-Blindness --DEAF-BLIND PERSPECTIVES, vol.5, #1, Fall 1997, pp.1-4.

Shane, Howard, Meghan O'Brien, and James Source. "Use of a Visual Graphic Language System to Support Communication for Persons on the Autism Spectrum." Perspectives (n.d.): n. pag. ASHA.org. ASHA. Web. <http://journals.asha.org/perspectivehttp://journals.asha.org/perspectives/terms.dtls/terms.dtl>.

Soto G, Zangari C. 2009. Practically speaking: Language, literacy, & academic development for students with AAC needs. Baltimore: Paul H. Brookes Publishing Co

Sturm, J., & Clendon, S. (2004). AAC, Language and Literacy. Topics in Language Disorders, 24, pp.76–91.

Thistle, J., & Wilkinson, K. M. (2009). The effects of foreground color and background color cues on typically developing preschoolers' speech of locating a target line drawing: Implication for AAC display design. American Journal of Speech-Language Pathology, 18, 231–240.

Vandervelden, M., & Siegel, L. (1999). Phonological processing and literacy in AAC users and students with motor speech impairments. Augmentative and Alternative Communication, 15, 191–211.

Vandervelden, M., & Siegel, L. (2001). Phonological processing in written word learning: Assessment for children who use augmentative and alternative communication. Augmentative and Alternative Communication, 17, 11–26.

Von Tetzchner, S. (1997) The use of graphic language intervention among young children in Norway. International Journal of Language & Communication Disorders Volume 32, Issue S3, pages 217–234, December 1997

Von Tetzchner S., Grove N., editors. (eds.). (2003). Augmentative and Alternative Communication. Developmental Issues. London: Whurr/Wiley

Vygotsky, L. "Thought and Language" MIT Press; (1986)

Wendt, Oliver, Schlosser, and Lyle Lloyd. AAC for Children with Autism; Proc. of ASHA, Philadelphia: n.p.,November 20, 2004

Wisconsin Assisitve Technology Initiative. (n.d.). Publications- Free materials. Retrieved from http://www.wati.org/?pageLoad=content/supports/free/index.php

Zabala, J. (2005). Ready, SETT, go! Getting started with the SETT framework. Closing the Gap, 23(6), 1-3.

Zabala, J. (2014). Sharing the SETT framework. Retrieved from http://www.joyzabala.com/

Zangari, C. Beyond Requesting: Thoughts on Teaching Interrogatives. PrAACtical AAC. February 16, 2013.

Additional References and Resources

American Speech-Language-Hearing Association. (2004). Roles and responsibilities of speech-language pathologists with respect to augmentative and alternative communication: Technical report [Technical Report]. Available from http://www.asha.org/policy

American Speech-Language-Hearing Assoc (2001a). *Competencies for speech-language pathologists providing services in augmentative communication.* Asha, 31(3), 107-110.

Banajee,M., DiCarlo, C., Striklin, S.B., (2003). Core vocabulary determination for toddlers. Augmentative and Alternative Communication, 19, 67-73.

Binger,C. & Light, J. (2007). *The effect of aided aac modeling on the expression of multisymbol messages by preschoolers who use aac. Augmentative and Alternative Communication*, 23(1), 30-43

Browder, D., Mims,P.; (2008). *Outcomes for Literacy for Students with Significant Cognitive Disabilities*, UNC-Charlotte

Browder,D., et al; Early Literacy Skills Builder. Attainment Co.

Burkhart,L., Costello, J. (2008). *CVI and complex communication needs: Characteristics and aac strategies.* CSUN. Los Angeles

Burkhart,L., Porter, G. (2006). *Partner assisted communication strategies for children who face multiple challenges.* ISAAC.

Caffiero,J., (2004). *AAC supports for engaging students with autism spectrum disorders in group instruction.* Closing the Gap.

Durand, V.M., (1999). *Functional Communication Using Assistive Devices;* Journal of Applied Behavior Analysis, 3 (3),247-267.

Finch, A. & Scherz,J. *Tips for Developing Literacy for Users of AAC;* Perspectives on AAC. 17 (2): 78 ASHA

Flippin,M., Reszka,S., & Watson,L. (2010). *Effectiveness of PECS on Communication & Speech for Children with Autism Spectrum Disorder*; American Journal of Speech-Language Pathology (February)

Goossens', Crain & Elder (1992). *Engineering the preschool environment for interactive, symbolic communication.* Southeast Augmentative Communication Conference Publications, as well as Mayer-Johnson Co.

Justice,L., et al (2010). *Print Focused Read Alouds in Preschool Classrooms*; LSHSS (April)

Kent-Walsh,J. & Binger,C. (2009) *Addressing the communication demands of the classroom for beginning communicators and early language users.* Practically Speaking: Language, Literacy, and Academic Development for Students with AAC Needs. Brookes Publishing.

Light,J. & McNaughton,D. (2007) *Evidence-Based Literacy Intervention for Individuals Who Require AAC.* ASHA. Boston

Musselwhite,C.R., Erickson,K., Zoilkowski,R. (2002). The Beginning Literacy Framework. Don Johnston Inc.

Musselwhite,C.R. (2006). R.A.P.S. *Writing Tips! Learning Magic Inc.*

Porter,G, & Caffiero, J. (2010). *PODD Communication Books: A Promising Practice for Individuals with Autism Spectrum Disorders.* Perspectives on AAC; ASHA.

Roman-Lantzy,C. (2007). *Cortical Visual Impairment: An Approach to Assessment and Intervention*. American Foundation for the Blind Press.

Sennett,S. & Bowker,A. (2010). *Autism, AAC, and Proloquo2Go.* Perspectives on AAC. ASHA.

Smith, M. (2009). *Vocabulary Instruction and Aided Communication.* AAC by the Bay Conference. San Francisco

Soto,G & Zangari,C. (2009). *Practically Speaking: Language, Literacy, and Academic Development for Students with AAC Needs*. Brookes Publishing.

Internet Resources:

www.aacinstitute.org Core vocabulary information

www.aacintervention.com Lots of information about AAC from where to start to literature based boards and tips and tricks. Musselwhite, C.

www.adaptivationinc.com Catalogue of devices, switches and more - fill out to whole citation w/ url

www.aren.scps.k12.fl.us/training/Flyers/ECT%20Intro.pdf Environmental Control Teaching manual

www.asha.org/docs ASHA's site contains position documents, and documents outlining their stand on the knowledge and skills, roles and responsibilities of slp's regarding aac

http://autismpdc.fpg.unc.edu Lists all evidence based practices for autism spectrum disorder; including overview, intervention steps, and check sheets

www.bcps.k12.md.us/boardmaker/adapted_library.asp Hundreds of books adapted with PCS-based communication boards. Each book has different levels of boards (usually 9 & 20 location grids). Can be used as communication boards or cut up for use in adapting books

http://boston.k12.ma.us/technology/emmanuel/ModifyingBooks.pdf - Pages of book ideas

www.candlelightstories.com Some ebooks are free, full access costs about $10

http://coefaculty.valdosta.edu/spe/ATRB/video - 2 minute video on ways to adapt books

www.creativecommunicating.com - Patti King-Debaun's website offers materials for teaching literacy to aac users

http://depts.washington.edu/enables/myths_aac_inter_infants.htm -
Website has good training information

www.enchantedlearning.com/Rhymes.html - $20 membership required.
for full site, but symbol adapted nursery rhymes free

www.lindaburkhart.com Offers a multitude of free handouts on
intervention in aac with students with complex communication needs,
cortical vision impairment, Rett syndrome, PODD communication books,
and more; as well as how-to handouts for building switches and mounts

www.dynavoxtech.com Look for Intervention Toolkit for handouts,
therapy ideas, and directions for activities

http://www.novita.org.au/Content.aspx?p=683 National Joint Committee
for the Communicative Needs of Persons with Severe Disabilities

www.paulakluth.com/articles Ideas for adapting books, including
students in general ed classrooms

www.pdictionary.com/ Internet picture dictionary provides symbols with
English and Spanish words for use in adapted books or communication
displays

http://prekese.dadeschools.net/resourcepages/resources_teacher_resourc
e_room_maint.htp - Resources for children's books, single-message
output, bilingual resources, overlay creating

www.prentrom.com Look for AAC Language Lab for step-by-step
intervention targets, IEP objectives, and plans. This is also the source for
the Pixon Project Kit by G. Van Tatenhove

www.storyplace.org%20 Charlotte & Mecklenburg County public library
has preschool stories with text, dialogue is highlighted, accompanying
games

http://trainland.tripod.com/pecs.htm - Links to many Boardmaker
overlays

http://aac.unl.edu/csl/pre.html Literacy, aac information

http://www.usu.edu/teachall/text/reading/Frylist.pdf Fry's instant sight word list - all 300

www.vantatenhove.com Gail has many handouts here on using core vocabulary, descriptive teaching, teaching Unity/Minspeak, and samples of the Pixon boards

Walter S. Gilliam & Paul B. de Mesquita (2006) The Relationship Between Language and Cognitive Development and Emotional-Behavioral Problems in Financially-Disadvantaged Preschoolers: A Longitudinal Investigation, Early Child Development and Care, 162:1, 9-24, DOI: 10.1080/0300443001620102

Deák, G.O. (2014). Interrelations of language and cognitive development. Encyclopedia of Language Development (pp. 284-291). P. Brooks & V. Kampe, Eds. SAGE

J Speech Hear Disord. 1980 Aug;45(3):408-14. **Election criteria for the adoption of an augmentative communication system: preliminary considerations.** Shane HC, Bashir AS.

The Relation between Age and Mean Length of Utterance in Morphemes Jon F. Miller and Robin S. Chapman 1980 JSLHR

Cole, K. N., Dale, P. S., & Mills, P. E. (1990). Defining language delay in young children by cognitive referencing: Are we saying more than we know? Applied Psycholinguistics, 11, 291–302.

Cole, K. N., Dale, P. S., & Mills, P. E. (1992). Stability of the intelligence quotient—language quotient relation: Is discrepancy modeling based on a myth? American Journal on Mental Retardation, 97(2), 131–143.

Lahey, M. (1990). Who shall be called language disordered? Some reflections and one perspective. Journal of Speech and Hearing Disorders, 55, 612–620.

Augmentative and Alternative Communication: Management of Severe Communication Disorders in Children and Adults

David R. Beukelman, Pat Mirenda P.H. Brookes Pub., Jan 1, 1998

Baker, Bruce, "Picturing Language: A 'How-To' Workshop," 2012.

Erickson, K. 2016 University of North Carolina at Chapel Hill, The Center for Literacy and Disability Studies www.project-core.com draft date: 09/25/2017

Nelson, C., van Dijk, J., Oster, T., McDonnell, A. Child-guided Strategies: The van Dijk Apprach to Assessment, American Printing House for the Blind, Inc. 2009

Adaptivation: sequencer:
https://docs.wixstatic.com/ugd/b1a4c2_01b9356096844698b45399a9e4 2fc6b0.pdf

randomizer:
https://docs.wixstatic.com/ugd/b1a4c2_ce0971a5d6da411dbdb42b62b1d 063fe.pdf

talking photo albums:
https://docs.wixstatic.com/ugd/b1a4c2_f8395cecb1aa42cd9fe0e9b475d0 a87f.pdf

Mervine, P. SpeakingOfSpeech.com
(https://speakingofspeechblog.wordpress.com)

https://pdhacademy.com/wp-content/uploads/2018/04/Vocabulary-Course-PDF.pdf

http://www.aacintervention.com/home/180009852/180009852/tips/2005 /01jan2005/colorcoding.pdf (for goosens, crane, elder)

Light J. "Shattering the silence": The development of communicative competence by individuals who require augmentative and alternative communication. Communicative competence for individuals who use augmentative and alternative communication, J. Light, D. Beukelman, J. Reichle. Paul H. Brookes, Baltimore, MD 2003; 3–38

Light J., Drager K. Maximizing language development with young children who require AAC. Seminar presented at the annual convention of the American Speech-ᵛ-Language-ᵛ-Hearing Association, San Diego,CA,2005

Gosnell, J., Costello, J., & Shane, H. (2011). Using a clinical approach to answer "What communication apps should we use?" *Augmentative and Alternative Communication*, 20, 87–96.

Cole, K. N., Dale, P. S., & Mills, D. E. (1990). Defining language delay in young children by cognitive referencing: Are we saying more than we know? Applied Psycholinguistics, 11, 291-302.

Cole, K. N., Dale, P. S., & Mills, P. E. (1992). Stability of the intelligence quotient—language quotient relation: Is discrepancy modeling based on a myth? American Journal on Mental Retardation, 97(2) 131-143.

Discrepancy Models and the Discrepancy Between Policy and Evidence (April 1996; 3:1). The Newsletter of Special Interest Division 1, Language Learning and Education. ASHA

Eligibility and Dismissal in Schools. http://www.asha.org/slp/schools/prof-consult/eligibility/

Lahey, M. (1990). Who shall be called language disordered? Some reflections and one perspective. Journal of Speech and Hearing Disorders, 55, 612-620.

Lahey, M. (1992). Linguistic and cultural diversity: Further problems for determining who shall be called language disordered. Journal of Speech and Hearing Disorders, 56, 638-639.

National Joint Committee for the Communication Needs of Persons With Severe Disabilities. (2003). Position statement on access to communication services and supports: Concerns regarding the application of restrictive "eligibility" policies [Position Statement]. Available from www.asha.org/policy or www.asha.org/njc.

Ourand, P. (2010). Cognitive Prerequisites Not Required for AAC Use. SpeechPathology.com; from AAC: Demystifying the "Assessment Process"

Special Education Eligibility: When Is a Speech-Language Impairment Also a Disability? Retrieved from http://leader.pubs.asha.org/article.aspx?articleid=2279030. (2011).

Terrell, F., Taylor, J., & Terrell, S. L. (1978). Effects of type of social reinforcement on the intelligence test performance of lower-class Black children. Journal of Consulting and Clinical Psychology, 46, 1538-1539.

Brown, L., Nietupski, J., & Hamre-Nietupski, S. (1976). The criterion of ultimate functioning in public school services for severely handicapped students. In M. A. Thomas (Ed.), Hey, don't forget about me: Education's investment in the severely, profoundly and multiply handicapped (pp. 2-15). Reston, V A: The Council for Exceptional Children.

Bronfenbrenner, V. (1979). The ecology of human development: Experiments by nature and design. Cambridge, MA: Harvard University Press.

Bruner, J. S. (1975). The ontogenesis of speech acts. Journal of Child Language, 2, 1-19.

Carr, E. (1985). Behavioral approaches to language and communication. In E. Schopler & G. Mesibov (Eds.), Current issues in autism: Vol. III. Communication problems in autism. New York: Plenum.

Hart, B., & Risley, T. R. (1975). Incidental teaching of language in the preschool. Journal of Applied Behavioral Analysis, 8, 411-420.

Lovaas, I. O. (1977). The autistic child. Irvington, NY: Irvington Press.

Miller, J. F., & Yoder, D. E. (1972). A syntax teaching program. In J. E. McLean, D. E. Yoder, & R. L. Schiefelbusch (Eds.), Language intervention with the retarded (pp. 191-211). Baltimore: University Park Press.

Light, J., & McNaughton, D. (2014). Communicative competence for individuals who require augmentative and alternative communication: A new definition for a new era of communication?. Augmentative and Alternative Communication, 30, 1- 18.

doi:10.3109/07434618.2014.885080

APPENDIX

Routines to build communication: AAC use in daily routines

Washing Hands: turn on, warm, not cold, put under, get wet, rub hands, rinse, dry, get towel, dry, hang up

- verbs: turn, put, get, rub, rinse, dry, hang

- prepositions: on, under, up

- adjectives: wet, dry, warm, cold (not)

- focus on targets: verbs or adjectives or prepositions, or simply apply ALgS

Eating snack: get snack, open lunchbox/bag, take out, open, help, eat, clean up, close, throw away, wipe

- verbs: get, open, close, wipe, eat, throw, help, clean, like

- prepositions: away

- adjectives: open, closed, clean, good,

- prepositions: in, out, up

Enter classroom - put away, hang up, take out (homework folder), sit down

- verbs: put, hang, take, sit

- prepositions: away, up, out, down
- adjectives & adverbs: quiet, quietly, noisy, quickly

Get dressed – put on, pull up, get them, put on, hurry, leg in, stand up

- verbs: put, pull, stand, push
- prepositions: in, out, up, down

Line up for recess/lunch/change room

- verbs: stand, make (a line), walk, go, open, close
- prepositions: inside, out, behind
- adjectives & adverbs: first, last, quiet, quickly

Calendar routines

- verbs: sit, put, help, say, sing, tell, point, count
- prepositions: there, in, on
- adjectives & adverbs: down, quietly, sunny, rainy, first, last

Bedtime routine

- verbs: dress/undress, brush, sleep, close, read
- prepositions: in/get in, on, under, between
- adjectives & adverbs: quickly, quietly, good

What kinds of toys build language?

This section is meant to be a starting point for knowing how to use toys to build your child's language.

The 'old-fashioned,' pre-technology toys are often some of the best toys for developing language skills, because they are more open ended and require some action or interaction.

The examples provided list ideas for building receptive language (understanding) and expressive language (spoken output or use of AAC system)

The following are covered: What type of toys to buy/use, how to think about what language skills to work on, and some examples for specific toy types.

- Look for open-ended play sets or toys that can be used multiple ways.

- Examples include kitchen play sets, farm or house play sets, building toys from blocks to Tinkertoys, themed play sets from pirates to space stations, dolls with accessories such as cars/changing tables/cradles/food sets, and more.

- Think about what you can do with them with your child.

  - Is there more than 1 way to use or play with this toy?

- Can I have my child follow or give directions? Ask or answer questions?

- Is there an opportunity for creating dialogue with this toy?

- Can my child construct a narrative around what (s)he is doing with the toy's parts or components?

- Can my child label/name the toy's parts and pieces? Name the function or action of the toy's pieces?

How do I think about what language to focus on?

- Think about your answers to the previous questions.

- Think about what your child is able to say now.

- Think about what (s)he should be able to say next; what's the next step in language development? {If needed, ask your child's teacher or speech therapist for ideas.}

- If your child can follow 1 step directions, then focus on 2-steps or 2 critical elements (such as 'the red ball' or 'the big red ball,' instead of just 'the ball.'

- If your child can answer What questions, but not What doing or Who or Where questions; then focus on asking those questions about what the figures are doing, or which figure is doing something, or which figure is where.

- If your child can name objects, but doesn't use descriptors, ask them to choose one of a group of items, then ask them to tell you which one they have; i.e. "the pink one." You might have to model it first; "Oh, you picked the pink one."

- If your child uses 2-3-word phrases, then focus on using simple complete sentences; such as, "I like this one," or "I see the dog," or "No, don't do that!" or "Put it here." Use high frequency words as much as possible rather than object names.

Ideas to get started

- Building blocks of any type:

- Receptive - Ask the child to find a block of a specific color or shape.

- Expressive - Ask the child to tell you the color or shape; to describe the block.

- Receptive - Ask the child to put a block in a specific location (on top, next to, etc.).

- Expressive - Ask the child to tell you where to put a block, or where he is going to put the next block.

- Receptive - Ask the child to follow a multiple critical element direction; such as 'put the big red block on top of this one,' or 'find the round blue block.'

- Expressive - Ask the child to tell you what he is doing; which one is picking and where it is going? Have him describe or narrate his actions

- Receptive - Ask a specific Wh question, where the child can point to the answer

- Expressive - Ask a specific Wh-question that the child needs to answer verbally

- Expressive - Tell me about what you built

Ideas to get started

- Play building of any type (house, farm, fire station, etc.)

- Receptive - Ask child to get a specific named object or figure.

- Expressive - Ask what object or figure the child wants you to get

- Receptive - Ask the child to put something in a specified location ('Put the baby in the bed.')

- Expressive - Ask the child to tell you where he is putting something.

- Receptive - Ask, "Can you make [figure] do X?" where X is an action.

- Expressive - Ask child to tell you what a figure is doing.

- Receptive - Ask the child to follow a multiple step or multiple critical elements direction with the figures or object in the play set; such as, "put the black sheep inside the barn," or, "put the sheep in the barn and the cow behind the barn,"

- Expressive - Ask the child to tell you what he is doing as he plays with the figures and pieces. Have him create a narrative of what he is doing.

- Receptive - Ask Wh-questions that can be answered by pointing or demonstrating with the play set pieces.

- Expressive - Ask a Wh-question to be answered verbally.

- Expressive - Have the child create a narrative or story about the play set and what he did.

ABC Communication Calendar

Monday	Tuesday	Wednesday	Thursday	Friday

Find an animal (real or stuffed). Can you find it in your AAC system? Find 1 word to describe it.

Find a favorite book. Tell 1 thing that's in the book.

Crazy Clothes - pick out a shirt & pants that don't match. Use your words to tell which ones you want.

Dance: tell someone how to move! Find the describing words in your aac system.

Emotions/ Feelings: Tell how you feel today. Find the words.

Pick a game to play: tell when it's your turn.

What makes you happy? Find the words in your AAC system.

What kind of ice cream do you like? Find the flavor in your AAC system.

Tell a joke. Don't know one? Say something kind to someone.

Tell something you like. Where is it in your AAC system?

Mine! Tell someone what is yours, what is theirs. Use "mine" and "yours."

Orange day: How many things can you name that are orange?

Have a picnic outside or in. What do you want to eat?

Rainbow day: Wear as many colors as you can. Pick them with the color words in your AAC system.

Act silly: What animal do you want to act like? What does it do?

What's your favorite time of day? What do you like to do then?

Find 3 things that are under something else. Tell someone what & where they are.

Watch a video. Tell something about your favorite part.

What is the weather like today?

Yellow: How many things can you name that are yellow? How does yellow make you feel?

ABC Communication Calendar

Monday	Tuesday	Wednesday	Thursday	Friday
a	b	c	d	e f
What animal do you like? Find it in your AAC system? Find 1 word to describe it.	Do you like bugs? Do you like bugs that fly or bugs that crawl?	What clothes do you wear in the summer? What do you wear in the winter?	Tell 3 things you do during the day you can't /don't do at night.	Emotions/ Feelings: Tell how you feel today. Find the words.
g	h	j	k	l
What gift would you like to get? Describe it.	Tell 3 things that make you happy.	How many times can you jump in place. Count with your AAC system?	Say something kind to someone.	Tell 3 things you like. Where are they in your AAC system?
m	n	p	r	s
Tell 2 things a monkey does. Find the words in your AAC system.	Say something nice to your mother.	Pigs, pickles, pie. Tell 1 word that describes each.	What is the rain like? Find the words in your AAC system.	What kind of sandwich do you like? Can you tell what you need to make it?
t	u	v	w	y
What's on top of your bed? On top of the table? On top of the desk?	Look up. What do you see in the clouds?	Watch a video. Tell something about your favorite part.	What is the weather like today?	Yikes! What scares you?

Taking Your AAC to the Beach

- School is out and summer fun is in. Your AAC user might not be getting the same level of intervention during the summer as (s)he gets during the school-year. But that shouldn't matter, because you know how to infuse AAC use into every-day activities, right? (Just wait till you turn the page!)

- I hope your AAC user has a good, robust AAC system to use all the time; however if it is an electronic system you might want to think twice about taking it for a swim. Electronic systems can be difficult to use at the beach or pool. Screens are difficult to see in the glare of the sun. (The industry has been getting better with this, but it's still a work-in-progress.) They also don't like sand or salt water very much. So, consider making a back-up communication book to take to the sea.

- Some of the dedicated device manufacturers have paper-based pages you can download from their websites. If you are using an iPad app, I recommend making a screen-shot of each page, printing them out, adding tabs to the edges of pages to label them - to make page turning/navigation easy.

- Ready to take your user, the book, and your beach gear to the water? Let's go!

- Core words to focus on:

- I/me, you, it

- dig, build, pour, put, give, help, turn, go, make

- in, on, over, on top, beside/next to, down,

- here, there, that

- more, all done, stop

- big, tall, deep, wet, little, lots, again

- where, what

- fun, happy, not like, yuck, uh oh

- yes, no

some fringe words:

sand, bucket/pail, shovel, water, castle, wave,

©susan berkowitz 2016

- We have identified the meaningful context to use: playing at the beach.

- You will set up the environment to best support the AAC user by using Aided Language Stimulation/Aided Input/consistent modeling.

  - Aided Language Stimulation is a strategy for teaching children to use AAC by having communication partners first provide picture-aided input to teach symbol meaning and word use using the AAC system simultaneously with speaking.

- You have made sure the child has an effective mode of communication: in this case a communication system (book, device, or activity based board as a last resort)

- You have chosen the appropriate vocabulary; choosing the core words associated with the activity and fringe vocabulary appropriate to the activity (see the previous page, and add vocabulary as appropriate for your child).

- You have included words to describe and talk about the activity, core action words needed within the activity, words to get more or to end the activity.

- You will get the child's attention, create the message with pictures, say the message, ask questions to increase the interaction. You will change the number of symbols you use, to be 1-2 more than the child uses/can do. You will match your pace to the child's ability to process. You will expand the child's responses, respond to everything, and keep the interaction going.

- And, finally, you have planned words and phrases to use within the activity, so that you are prepared:

  - My turn, you do it, fill it, pour it, turn it over, do it again, build it, put here, get more, wet, make higher, do more, build more, fill it more, dig here, no water, more sand, put on top, put next to, do over, dig under, need more, all done

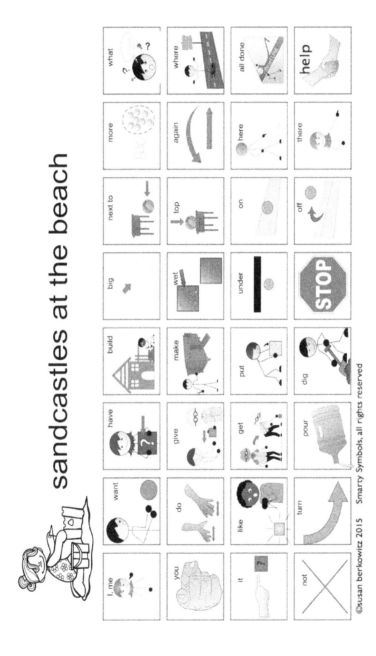

- These are meant as a starting point to give you some ideas for how to plan activities for AAC users when you are just starting out. You will find that as you become more comfortable with both your AAC users' AAC systems and with the practice of ALgS or AI that you no longer need to plan or map out activities; unless you are planning a complicated activity or shared book reading.

- With shared reading and AAC users, you will find that there are times when, rather than reading the story as it was written, you want to re-write it based on core vocabulary use. Use short, well-known folk- and fairy-tales. For young children, use Nursery Rhymes. (Note: they will probably not rhyme once you substitute core words, but that's ok.)

Aided Language Stimulation (ALgS) is a crucial step in the process of teaching a child to use AAC, as I've said before (and may say again). It is used in order to:

- increase the child's exposure to a variety of vocabulary, across different communicative functions, in genuine, natural contexts,

- increase the child's comprehension of language concepts with clear structure; establishing associations,

- provide a format for all communication partners to learn the concept of modeling (as well as to become familiar with the AAC system).

Identify potential target vocabulary within specified activities/ contexts. Select vocabulary to target. Provide ALgS/Modeling. Use expectant pauses, natural cues. Collecting data doesn't need to be elaborate or difficult. Keep it simple.

One way to plan basic activity language to model:

| What does he like/love (to do)? |

| Words used to describe the activity | | Words used to talk about the activity |

| Core words used in the activity (think verbs, adjectives, pronouns; what do you do with it?) Teach these first |

| Action words used in the activity | | Words to get more | | Words to stop |

- Another way to plan is to list, on a spreadsheet, the activities or routines that happen, then list in the next column, who the communication partner is likely to be, next list possible core words for that activity (i.e. put in, want more, you do, etc.), then list what words you might use to model; making a column each for single word/symbol, 2-symbol phrase, 3-symbol phrase.

- There is no need to go beyond 3-word phrases for early communicators unless they are beginning to use beginning phrases consistently.

bubbles

· Possible Partners: parent, sibling, classroom aide, speech therapist

· Possible vocabulary: blow bubbles, big, small, lots, more, high, catch, pop, there, want, you, do, it, me, my, turn, like, fun, feel, not

· Possible Single Word Targets: blow, more, big, small, pop, catch, there, want, you, do, me, like, not (or, more simplified: blow, more, pop, want, like)

· Possible Two-word Targets: blow bubbles, more bubbles, my turn, you do, blow more, catch it, pop it, me like, me want, want more, not like, no more, all done (or, more simplified: want more, you do, pop it, all done, blow more)

Mr. Potato Head

- Possible Partners: parent, sibling, classroom aide, speech therapist
- Possible vocabulary: put, there, want, you, do, it, me, my, turn, like, fun, feel, not, that, these, again, push, in, on, more, all done, look
- Possible Single Word Targets: put, it, there, want, need, you, do, me, like, not, different (or, more simplified: put, that, like, there, different)
- Possible Two-word Targets: put it, push it, put in, put on, my turn, you do, do more, put again, get different, me like, me want, want more, not like, no more, all done (or, more simplified: want that, you do, put it, all done, put on)

Play Dough

- Possible Partners: parent, sibling, classroom aide, speech therapist
- Possible vocabulary: put, more, there, want, look, you, do, it, me, my, turn, like, fun, feel, not, that, these, again, push, in, on, roll, push, (color names)
- Possible Single Word Targets: put, it, get, there, want, need, you, do, me, like, not, different, roll, push (or, more simplified: get, that, like, roll, different)
- Possible Two-word Targets: put it, push it, put in, put on, my turn, you do, do more, roll again, get different, me like, me want, want more, not like, no more, all done (or, more simplified: want that, you do, put it, all done, push it or roll it)

Make Up

- Possible Partners: mom, sibling, classroom aide, speech therapist
- Possible vocabulary: put, there, want, you, do, it, me, my, turn, like, fun, feel, not, that, these, again, on, brush (v), wet, dry, more, look, (color names)
- Possible Single Word Targets: put, it, get, there, want, need, you, do, me, like, not, different, brush, more (or, more simplified: want, that, like, color, different, more)
- Possible Two-word Targets: put it, different one, put on, my turn, you do, do more, get different, me like, me want, want more, not like, no more, all done (or, more simplified: want that, you do, put it, all done, do more)

Sports Re-play

- Possible Partners: dad, sibling, classroom aide, speech therapist, coach/PE teacher

- Possible vocabulary: look, he, do, hit, push, throw, catch, kick, run, fall, they, I, you, see, it, that, here, there, win, lose, all done, watch, different, go, more, jump, stop, what? who? where?

- Possible Single Word Targets: look, watch, hit, go, stop, more, fall, throw/kick/hit/run/jump, different, win, not, who? where? (or, more simplified: watch, that, like, who?)

- Possible Two-word Targets: put it, throw it, put in, he/they do, me like, not like, no more, all done (or, more simplified: watch that, they do, he put, all done)

Being a Good Communication Partner

Good communication partners create a positive communication environment, respond to all communication attempts, and use the child's AAC system to communicate with them.

There is a positive communication environment when we respond to all of a child's communication attempts, provide support as needed, focus on positive results and successes, and find solutions to challenges.

Even when you respond to an undesirable behavior, if you do so while also modeling how to use a correct message in the AAC system you take advantage of a communication opportunity.

As much as possible, do not ask yes/no questions and do not ask closed questions. These are dead end communication responses, and they do not lead to further interaction and communication most of the time. Nor do they foster communication growth.

Do ask Wh-Questions, or any other open-ended questions. If necessary, use multiple choice questions. Then follow-up on the response.

Strategies to create opportunities to communicate include providing choices, sabotaging the environment, giving small amounts, briefly delaying access, using pause time, and fill-in-the-blank activities.

Making choices is an early-developing communication function and allows the child the opportunity to make a communication response.

Sabotaging the environment – for example holding the book up-side-down, giving the wrong choice, putting a preferred item out of reach – provide more opportunities for communicating.

All children communicate. They don't all communicate symbolically – that is, with words, pictures, text. And some of their non-symbolic communication is undesirable. Some children are frustrated enough to use aggressive, destructive, or self-injurious behaviors.

Think about how your child responds to his/her own name; what (s)he does when the routine is interrupted; what (s)he does when wanting an item, action, escape, or help; tells you when something is wrong.

What I'm talking about is how this child communicates to reject/protest, request, comment. Those are some of the functions of communication we see most often.

What communication partners need to do is to respond to those other communication behaviors while shaping them into more acceptable or understandable forms.

The more you practice using the AAC system during real contexts, and increase the number of contexts in which you use the AAC system, the more automatically the child will learn to use the AAC system.

Use the AAC system to communicate TO the child. Aided Language Stimulation (also called Partner Aided Input or Aided Input) is crucial to the child learning to use AAC.

- Language is learned through models.
- Children learn spoken language by listening to others use it.
- A child using picture-based communication is learning an entirely different language.
- This child needs to see models of people using the picture-based system effectively. And models provided in response to his communication are the most powerful.

In order to facilitate communication in AAC users we need to do several things consistently:

- Provide access to the AAC system. It needs to be available all the time. This is how the child "talks" and he needs to know that communication is valued enough to be there whenever it is needed – not just at a specified activity time.
- Provide AAC models. Use aided language input as much as possible. When asking questions, highlight key words by using AAC.
- Provide opportunities for the child to take a turn; such as by pausing after each turn you take. Don't be the only one communicating. Don't do all the 'talking.'
- Pause. Use expectant delay. Give the child time to process and time to formulate a response. Looking expectantly while pausing lets the child know you expect a response.
- Ask open-ended questions and wait for the answer before you provide it. If necessary, you can answer the question, then provide a cue or prompt for the child to imitate the answer.

Asking Wh-questions instead of yes/no questions allows the child the opportunity to learn higher level responses.
- Prompt those responses. Providing verbal prompts lets the child know what they are supposed to do.

When do I do each of these things?

Begin with routine activities. Many routine activities have a set beginning – middle – ending that are predictable, and use words predictably. This makes it easier for the child.

Some other activities are less predictable, but can easily provide communication opportunities.

Start with one activity. When you feel comfortable, add another.

Keep adding activities throughout the day until the strategies are being used all of the time.

Keep track of the need for new vocabulary.

By the time you have increased the number of contexts you might find there is more vocabulary needed in the AAC system. These are the times to uncover those previously hidden buttons.

Have a plan for how to keep track of this. For example, keep a list on a clipboard where words can be written down as they come up, before the partner forgets.

- Core Word Roll and Fill-in is an activity for decontextualized core word practice with AAC systems, but can also be used with other emerging communicators who need to practice expanding their responses/utterances.

- There are 24 core words represented on the dice.

- The objective of this activity is for AAC users to use the core word rolled on the die to:

    1. find the word in their AAC system,

    2. create a 2-3-word phrase using that core word, or

    3. create a simple sentence using that core word.

For the next step in creating core word phrases and sentences, try Core Vocabulary Roll a Sentence Practice.

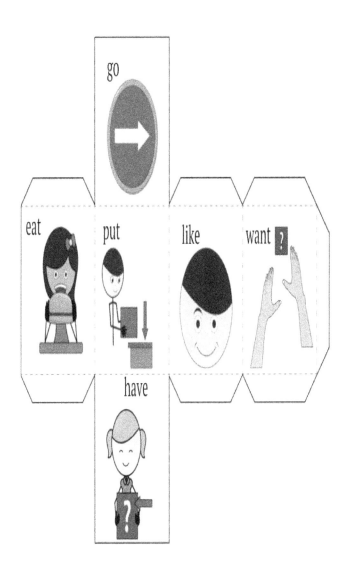

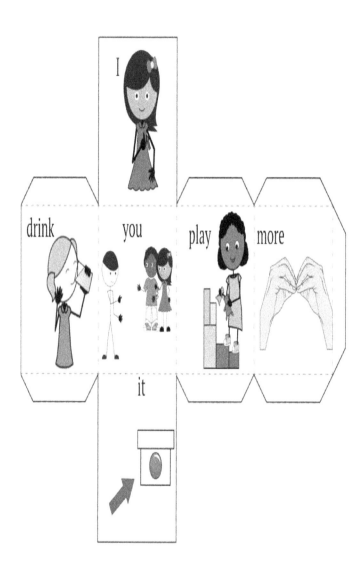

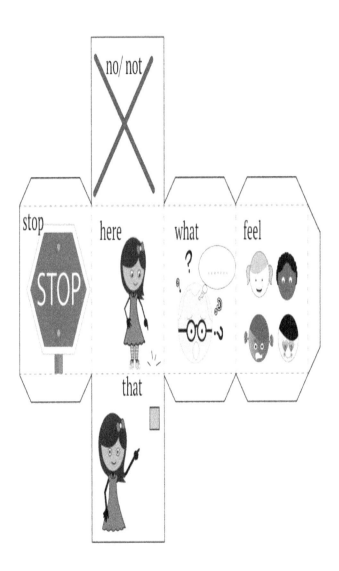

Figures

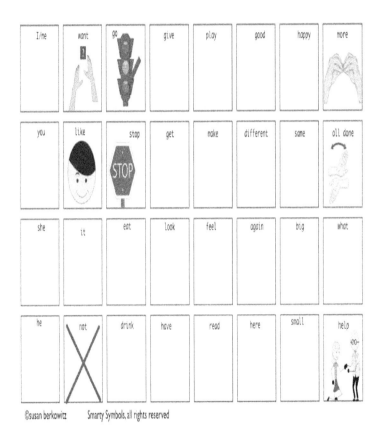

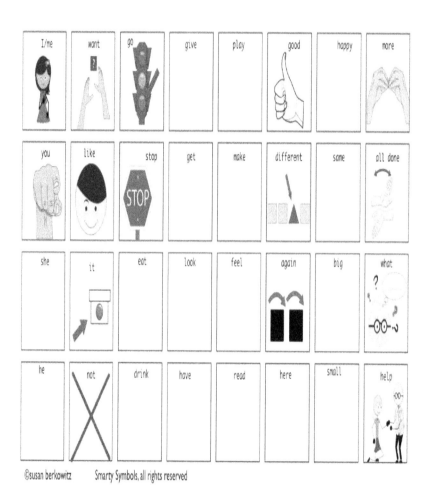

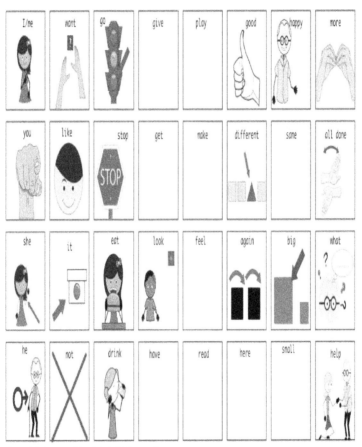

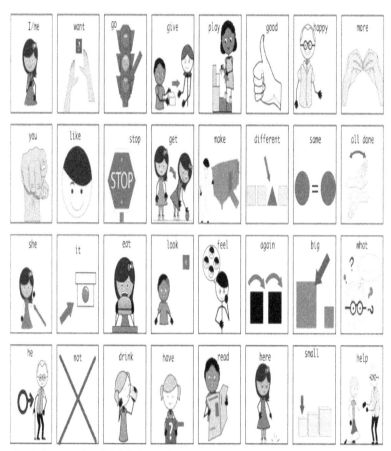

clip art credits

Susan Berkowitz has been a Speech Language Pathologist for more than 40 years, during which time she has concentrated predominantly on Augmentative and Alternative Communication, AAC; except for 8 years working in a school district with significantly language-learning disabled students K-8. She has worked for more than 45 years with students with autism. Susan has extensive background in psychology, special education, speech pathology and audiology, school administration, and Applied Behavior Analysis.

She has worked as a practitioner, supervisor, Director of the Communication Department, and Director of Education. Susan's clinical experience has included public and non-public schools, non-profit community agencies, residential settings, and her own private practice. She has been published in peer-reviewed professional journals, and presented at national and international conferences; including ASHA, ATIA, CSUN, CTG, and the Annual ABA Conference.

Susan has provided professional training to school district staffs in California and Massachusetts on Inclusion, implementation of AAC, Scope and Implementation of Assistive Technology, Working with Students on the Spectrum, and more. She has recently completed a book, "Make the Connection," providing how-to advice for parents and SLPs new to AAC.

Susan holds certification in Mobile Technology for Students with Disabilities and the Wisnia-Kapp Reading Program, in addition to her Clinical Cs and licenses and classroom certifications.

Susan Berkowitz received her B.A. in psychology from Clark University, her M.S. in Speech-Pathology and Audiology from Tulane, and an M.Ed. in Education Administration from California State University at Fullerton.

She also creates and sells adapted special education and AAC curricular materials on her website https://susanberkowitz.net and on https://www.teacherspayteachers.com/Store/Susan-Berkowitz

https://tinyurl.com/AAC-AppendixLink

For more information please go to

website: https://susanberkowitz.net

email: languagelearningapps@gmail.com

In one book Susan gets you from barely knowledgeable to comfortable with AAC. This is a book for every professional and parent working with a student using iPads and other technology to communicate.

— Nydia Celina Viloria, Parent

This book is the tool that allows you to shorten your learning curve and better serve your clients or children who use AAC, a must for anyone expanding communication through technology.

— SM, Parent

Feel comfortable giving competent advice and recommendations about AAC. Understand the breadth and depth of the resources available as well as their use and shine at your next IEP.

— ML, Parent

As a parent embarking on a journey to support your child with communication needs, this book will guide you through a deep understanding of AAC, its use and its implementation. A must for every parent trying to shorten their learning curve!

— KO, Parent

Even seasoned professionals will find jewels of information in Susan's book, a much-needed resource to round out your knowledge as you work with students on AAC.

— DT, Parent